Grounds Maintenance

Grounds Maintenance

A contractor's guide to competitive tendering

PHILIP SAYERS

E. & F.N. SPON

An imprint of Chapman and Hall

LONDON · NEW YORK · TOKYO · MELBOURNE · MADRAS

UK   Chapman and Hall, 2–6 Boundary Row, London SE1 8HN

USA   Van Nostrand Reinhold, 115 5th Avenue, New York NY10003

JAPAN   Chapman and Hall Japan, Thomson Publishing Japan, Hirakawacho Nemoto Building, 7F, 1-7-11 Hirakawa-cho, Chiyoda-ku, Tokyo 102

AUSTRALIA Chapman and Hall Australia, Thomas Nelson Australia, 480 La Trobe Street, PO Box 4725, Melbourne 3000

INDIA   Chapman and Hall India, R. Seshadri, 32 Second Main Road, CIT East, Madras 600 035

First edition 1991

© 1991 Philip Sayers

Typeset in 10/12 pt Palatino by Best-set Typesetter Ltd
Printed in Great Britain by T.J. Press (Padstow) Ltd, Padstow, Cornwall

ISBN 0 419 15510 4 (HB)   0 442 31304 7 (USA)

British Library Cataloguing in Publication Data
Sayers, Philip
   Grounds maintenance: Contractor's
   guide to competitive tendering
   1. Great Britain. Outdoor recreation
   facilities. Maintenance. Contracts
   I. Title
   769.06841

ISBN 0-419-15510-4

Library of Congress Cataloging-in-Publication Data
Sayers, Philip, 1945–
   Grounds maintenance: a contractor's guide to competitive
tendering / Philip Sayers. — 1st ed.
     p. cm.
   Includes bibliographical references and index.
   ISBN 0-419-15510-4
   1. Contracts for work and labor — Great Britain. 2. Grounds
maintenance industry — Law and legislation — Great Britain.
I. Title.
KD1638.S29 1991
343.41'07659—dc20   90-19180
[344.1037659]   CIP

Contents

Preface

The Local Government Act, 1988, has completely changed the basis for the provision of many maintenance services provided by public authorities. It has opened up a whole area of work to competitive tendering. Grounds maintenance especially is being changed from anything previously known.

Gone are the days when local and public authorities could undertake most of their own grounds maintenance works using their in-house 'direct workforce'; without comparison of cost. Gone are the days when the only contracts put out to tender were those for highway grass-cutting, large tree surgery and new landscaping works.

The guidelines contained within this book provide a step by step approach to each stage of the competitive tendering process and are valid for contractors both in the private and public sector.

The book gives valuable information and advice for the benefit of directors, managers and foremen, contractors, public authority direct works teams and students. It is of particular value to all those seeking information, or wishing to succeed, in the increasingly competitive market of public authority service provision.

Although the book relates to grounds maintenance, the principles discussed in the book are equally applicable to other competitive tender situations.

The author is grateful for the information and assistance given in preparing the book, and especially to those listed in the Acknowledgements and reference section at the end.

Whilst every care has been taken in researching and preparing the book, the author offers the information for guidance only without creating any legal liability. He would welcome any comments.

The male pronoun is used in the book. This is for ease of reading and should be taken to mean both male and female individuals.

Chapter One

The tender documents

INTRODUCTION

The tender documents produced by public authorities are large, detailed and doubtless, for the newcomer, intimidating.

Tender documents may also seem formidable to experienced companies and to the grounds maintenance sections of many local authorities. They are large and highly detailed, due to the fact that they contain all the necessary information for a three- to six-year contract.

The guidelines contained in this book aim to highlight all the key issues, and they should be particularly helpful in the stages prior to submitting a tender. They should also be of help to those who wish to be well-informed about the whole approach to grounds maintenance – from the contractor's point of view.

Local authorities throughout the country regularly invite competent interested persons to tender for their grounds maintenance operations by public advertisement. At the time the advertisement appears, the authority will have available copies of their current grounds maintenance tenders. They are freely provided to read in their offices, or available for purchase.

Most local authorities will advertise a proportion of their grounds maintenance works each year. Such advertisements appear both in the local and specialist national press.

The advertisement will seek persons willing and able to **tender** a price (or prices) for the horticultural works specified. However some may well consider that the term 'tender' relates to the sinking feeling experienced on seeing the size of an average tender document!

After reading a tender, an appointment with a solicitor may appear to be the next best step (or alternatively, a stiff drink!). Yet there is little value in speaking so early to a legal adviser. It is always advisable to wait awhile, and re-read the document in a day or two. Professional legal advice never comes cheap.

Fig. 1.1   Reading it will make you feel tender

PROFESSIONAL ADVICE

Here there is a key difference in approach between two of the principal competitors. Public authorities will tend to seek professional advice readily in their bids to be successful in tender submissions. But even a local authority grounds maintence section has to pay for legal and accountancy services – and even when supplied within that authority itself.

Many smaller companies will choose not to incur such costs at this early stage. At the start of the tendering process, it is necessary only to express an interest in an authority's tender. That should not require legal advice, nor prove too difficult. Many contractors who enter this field of work for the first time will make a number of submissions for different contracts to a number of different authorities.

Experience is always a good teacher. But in addition to experience, a knowledge of the background to competitive tendering will be helpful.

THE STARTING-POINT

Each tender document has been compiled as required by the Local Government Act 1988 (and subsequent government Orders and Directives). For those wishing to look into the background more fully, the Act is readily available in public libraries; and the References at the end of this book provide further information which should be useful. Some brief extracts of the Act, together with subsequent government Orders, are given in the next few pages.

Local Government Act 1988

1988 CHAPTER 9

An Act to secure that local and other public authorities undertake certain activities only if they can do so competitively; to regulate certain functions of local and other public authorities in connection with public supply or works contracts; to authorise and regulate the provision of financial assistance by local authorities for certain housing purposes; to prohibit the promotion of homosexuality by local authorities; to make provision about local authorities' publicity, local government administration, the powers of auditors, land held by public bodies, direct labour organisations, arrangements under the Employment and Training Act 1973, the Commission for Local Authority Accounts in Scotland, the auditing of accounts of local authorities in Scotland, and dog registration, dog licences and stray dogs; and for connected purposes. [24th March 1988]

BE IT ENACTED by the Queen's most Excellent Majesty, by and with the advice and consent of the Lords Spiritual and Temporal, and Commons, in this present Parliament assembled, and by the authority of the same, as follows:—

Fig. 1.2   The need to compete is stated clearly at the beginning of the Act

Appeals

Appeals are allowed to the secretary of state if there is reason to believe that the tender is unfair or does not accord with the Act and regulations, or if the tender is attempting to be anti-competitive.

For those who are familiar with tenders and believe that a tender is unfair, then they will undoubtedly use the appeal procedure. Relative newcomers to tendering will be better advised to direct their energies to ensuring that the best possible tender submission is made.

The legislation has been enacted to bring the perceived benefits of competition to local authority operated services. The need to compete is clearly stated at the beginning of the Act; this is competition, not privatization: maintenance at the least cost is the goal. Anyone involved in the competition needs to establish this goal at the outset – then the best will win.

Some say standards suffer. Well, perhaps, they do – but often that will be as much the fault of the client as the contractor.

THE METHOD

The tendering process can be seen simply in the following steps:

1. The local authority advertises its intention to let a grounds mainten-ance contract and invites interested persons to contact its offices.
2. The local authority assesses the relative abilities of those applying.
3. A shortlist of competent contractors is compiled.
4. Only those on the shortlist are then invited to tender for the actual works.
5. On receipt of the returned tenders, the local authority will determine the best bid, and award the contract.

The Tender Documents prepared by the authority form the basis of everything to do with the tendering procedure and the subsequent contract.

KEY TERMS

Before looking at the tender documents, it is worth listing a few of the more common terms used in tendering documents:

- The **tender** – the package of documents supplied by the authority which details all the works, and how such works will be carried out.
- The **tenderer** – the person who completes the tender and returns it to the authority (e.g. a landscape contractor).
- The **contractor** – the person who submits the winning tender and is awarded the contract (thus becoming the contractor).
- The **client** – the authority (and its officers), who award and run the contract.

In the next part of the chapter, each section of the tender document is looked at in turn. An outline tender document is provided in Appendix A1 at the end of the book.

CONDITIONS OF TENDER AND OF CONTRACT

The Conditions of Tender are the simplest part of the document. They simply state how, when and where the tender is to be submitted. This usually means submitting the completed tender back to the authority in a plain sealed envelope, by the stated date. Be warned, all tenders should be returned early, even one minute late is too late.

The Conditions of Contract section is much more substantial (and can be overwhelming). These conditions need very careful reading, for the winning contractor will be bound by them for the duration of the contract.

At the stage of expressing an interest in a contract, there is really no need yet to seek legal advice, provided that the conditions are understandable. However, expert legal advice is essential when the time arrives to submit a tender.

At that time, it is always advisable for a solicitor with relevant previous experience to be involved. It is also important to establish legal charges at the outset.

The principal advice here is to be economical with the (expensive) time of legal and other professionals. This is equally valid for the public sector contractor seeking to submit a bid as for the private contractor. The familiar adage, *check cost before commitment . . .* is an excellent one.

The conditions of contract are the terms by which the local authority will enforce the contract. Local authorities need to give themselves adequate powers of control over such things as:

- hours of the day when work is allowed;
- insurance and indemnity;
- an adequate financial bond to safeguard the performance of the contract;
- default procedures and termination clauses;
- provision for annual inflation increases;
- and a host of other matters.

From the contractor's point of view, these conditions will influence working methods and costing, so it is vitally important to assess the extent of their impact. Anyone submitting a bid needs to ensure that they will be able to comply with **all** the conditions. The winning contractor will be bound by them.

THE SPECIFICATION

The next section of a tender document may well deal with the Specification. Here will be itemized all the well-known grounds maintenance tasks to be carried out. Real horiticulture at last!

Of course, the document will say nothing as straightforward as 'Look after the bowling green for a year'. All the tasks will be minutely itemized to specify the type of machinery to the used, the frequency and height of cutting, the time of day by which the task should be completed, and so on.

The Specification section, then, demands careful reading. Each aspect of work will need to be costed on the basis of the stipulated requirements. In the event of a dispute, it is the Specification which will be minutely scrutinized. Also, in a dispute, the Conditions of Contract, will be of fundamental importance.

The section dealing with the Bills of Quantity details the quantity of work to be undertaken. Here, the tenderer will be required to state his prices.

SCHEDULE OF RATES

The Schedule of Rates will follow. At this stage, anyone submitting a tender will need to state his prices. Normally the Schedule of Rates will be for tasks required to be undertaken only occasionally. The quantity of work specified in this section is usually very small, because the actual works will be ordered individually as required by the client.

THE RIGHT PRICE AND SUBMISSION

For the tenderer, the submission of the prices (or rates) for each item will be of prime consideration: once stated, never varied. Well, almost never: exceptions would include the annual increase for inflation, and any variations agreed with the authority.

The tender will need to state his rates in the blank columns (Table 1.1). It will be clearly shown in the tender document where the rates should be inserted. Some tenders require the rates to be stated in the Schedule of Rates or in the Bills of Quantity or in a separate section.

At the end of the tender document, there will be a number of appendices, including:

- timescales and programme for works;
- maps and plans;
- forms of agreement.

The appendices, like the tender documents themselves, will vary. Even though these details have been relegated to an appendix, they still

Table 1.1 An example of completing a tender

No.	Specification	Quantity	Rate (£)
1.	*Hedge cutting:* Cut cleanly all hedges with approved equipment, to a height of 5 ft, 4 ft, wide, with straight top and sides. Rake out all debris from under the hedge, and dispose of to tip with all arisings from the work. Leave site clean and tidy at the end of each working day	lin. m	This column to be completed by the tenderer, e.g. £100
2.	*Bedding plants – supply:* Supply good-quality bedding plants to the satisfaction of the Supervising Officer and in accordance with British Standard Specification No. 3936, Part 7, 1989	per 1000	
3.	*Bedding plants – plant:* Remove all old plants from bed to tip. Fork the ground to 9 in, cultivate to tilth. Plant approved plants. Plant 9 plants per square metre	100 m^2	

require most careful study. Such details are obtained as well for the four to six years of the contract.

Once a prospective contractor has read and fully considered the tender documents, they will be ready to complete the forms and return them by the given date and time to the local authority. If successful, the completed document will form the basis of a binding legal contract. Critical attention to every part of the document is therefore essential.

SUMMARY

To help us summarize this chapter, a number of key points need to be emphasized, as follows:

- Public authority grounds maintenance is the subject of open competition.
- The Local Government Act 1988, and subsequent regulations, will govern the operation of the tender procedure.
- The tender documents are easy to obtain.

Fig. 1.3 Advertisements appear in local newspapers and the specialist press

- Local authorities will provide a copy of their tender documentation to read free of charge, when the tender is advertised.
- Tenders are big; they are easier to understand when taken section by section:
  - tender conditions relate to the submission of the tenders (e.g. return all tenders by 12 noon on a given date);
  - contract conditions relate to the subsequent contract (e.g. no working after 7.00 pm);
  - work specifications detail the actual work to be carried out (e.g. 'hedge top – cut square');
  - quantities of work (e.g. two bowling-greens, 1000 m of hedge);
  - rates are left blank – prices to be inserted by tenderer;
  - there will be other sections which the authority considers necessary.
- Limited free advice may sometimes be available from the local authority or local business advice centre (or even a local solicitor or accountant, as a gesture of goodwill).
- For the successful tenderer, the tender document will form the basis of a binding legal agreement, lasting up to six years.

Once a tender document is broken down into its various parts, understanding becomes easier. For anyone starting out on competitive tendering, it is always wise to glance through at least half a dozen tender documents from different authorities. There is no better way of testing the temperature of the water.

ADDENDUM: SOME GOVERNMENT DIRECTIVES

This addendum gives some fundamental guidelines instituted by the government; they are reproduced with the permission of the Controller of Her Majesty's Stationery Office. We include here an extract from the Local Government Act 1988 and Department of the Environment Circulars 8/88 and 19/88.

The definition of grounds maintenance is succinctly stated in the Act itself. Indeed, it is amazing that the purpose of a whole industry can be summarized in so few words. The Act states that the maintenance of ground is:

- cutting and tending grass (including re-turfing and re-seeding but not intitial turfing or seeding);
- planting and tending trees, hedges, shrubs, flowers and other plants (but excluding landscaping any area);
- controlling weeds.

Specifically excluded is any activity where the primary purposes is research or securing the survival of any species of plant. There have been additions to this list, by way of government circulars and guidelines.

Two of the more important circulars are reproduced, in part, here. They refer to the procedures for tendering, specifically mentioning details of relevance to grounds maintenance tenders, and the financial return required to be achieved by local authorities.

Circular 8/88
(Department of the Environment)

Circular 12/88
(Welsh Office)

Joint Circular from the

Department of the Environment

2 Marsham Street London SW1P 3EB

Welsh Office

Cathays Park Cardiff CF1 3NQ

6 April 1988

Local Government Act 1988—Public Supply and Works Contracts: Non-Commercial Matters

1.   We are directed by the Secretary of State for the Environment and the Secretary of State for Wales to refer to the Local Government Act 1988, which received Royal Assent on 24 March, 1988. Part II of the Act, which deals with public supply and works contracts, comes into force on 7 April, 1988; its provisions apply to local authorities and to other public bodies listed in Schedule 2 to the Act (the "authorities"). These are set out in Annex A. This circular is addressed to local authorities and other public bodies in England and Wales.

2.   The purpose of this circular is to give guidance on the Part II provisions and to promulgate specified questions and descriptions of evidence under Section 18(5). Further guidance will be issued on the Act's other provisions in due course.

Exclusion of Non-Commercial Considerations

3.   Part II of the Act is designed to prevent the authorities from discriminating against particular contractors by introducing political or other irrelevant considerations into the contractual process.

4.   Section 17 requires the authorities to exercise their public supply or works contract functions without reference to the non-commercial matters specified in Section 17(5). Public supply or works contracts are contracts for the supply of goods or materials, the supply of services or the execution of works, but Section 17 does not apply to any such contracts entered into before 7 April, 1988.

5.   The contractual functions covered by Section 17 are:

(a) the inclusion or exclusion of anybody from a list of approved contractors or lists of persons from whom tenders are invited;

(b) the acceptance or non-acceptance of tenders;

(c) the selection of the successful contractor;

(d) the approval, non-approval, selection and nomination of sub-contractors for proposed or existing contracts; and

(e) the termination of a contract.

Non-Commercial Matters

6.   The non-commercial matters are listed in Section 17(5), and further defined in Section 17(8). They include such matters as rates of pay, the area of residence of the workforce, the number or proportion of apprentices or women to be employed and the number of ethnic minority employees (but see paragraphs 10–13 below). Bans on contractors who use self-employed labour-only sub-contractors, who have worked on nuclear missile sites or whose vehicles have crossed picket lines are no longer permissible. Any links which a contractor or his associated companies have with a particular country or territory must not be taken into account, nor should membership of bodies such as trade associations or links with freemasonry be considered. Enquiries about contributions to political parties or requests for donations to social projects are not allowed, and insistence that approval of work under the Building Regulations must be given by the local authority, rather than, say, the National House Building Council, will no longer be permitted. It should be noted that matters which are non-commercial in relation to a contractor are also non-commercial in relation to those persons associated with the contractor who are mentioned in Section 17(7).

7.   However, it is not the intention to prevent reasonable enquiries of contractors about their workforce where the background and character of employees is an important functional factor in work of a sensitive nature, such as work with children. In such circumstances, questions as to whether character references are taken up, or requests for names and addresses where appropriate, are considered to be about management systems rather than 'composition of the workforce'.

8.   It has never been the Government's intention to prevent authorities taking account of contractors' health and safety records during the contractual process. Whilst the Government would want questions kept to the minimum necessary, there is no reason why authorities should not make reasonable enquiries about contractors' health and safety records and their arrangements for making their employees aware of their health and safety obligations. Furthermore, whilst questions about training arrangements are not permitted, authorities are not prevented from asking questions about the qualifications of a contractor's workforce, or from requiring that particular kinds of work are carried out by people holding appropriate qualifications.

9.   Although Section 17(5)(f) covers membership of organisations such as employers' or trade associations, authorities will not be prevented from requiring that work should be carried out to certain standards, e.g. that gas or electrical installations are carried out in accordance with standards laid down by the regulatory bodies for those industries. Nor does Section 17 prevent authorities insisting that work is covered by appropriate guarantees, which are, of course, often provided through membership of an employers' or trade association.

Race Relations Matters

10.   The one area where local authorities are allowed under the Act to take account of non-commercial matters during the contractual process is in the

field of race relations. This is in view of the fact that Section 71 of the Race Relations Act 1976 places a duty on local authorities to ensure that their various functions are carried out with due regard to the need to eliminate unlawful racial discrimination and to promote equality of opportunity, and good relations, between persons of different racial groups.

11.   Section 18 of the Act therefore allows local authorities to ask approved written questions and include terms in a draft contract which relate to the workforce matters in Section 17(5)(a) if it is reasonably necessary to do so to secure compliance with Section 71. Authorities who decide to ask such questions should do so at the pre-contract stage, since subsisting contracts may not be terminated as a result of such enquiries.

12.   Section 18(5) provides that the Secretary of State shall specify the written questions and descriptions of evidence which are to be approved for these purposes. Following consultation with the Commission for Racial Equality, the Confederation of British Industry, the local authority associations and other interested bodies, the Secretary of State has exercised the power conferred by Section 18(5) to specify the questions and the description of evidence set out in Annex B to this circular. It should be noted that the request for examples to illustrate the answer to the fifth question is the only approved description of evidence.

13.   The provisions of Section 18 obviously have no effect outside the contractual process and authorities are not prevented from promoting good race relations practices in their area, for example through meetings with local employers.

Duty to Give Reasons for Decisions

14.   Section 20 of the Act requires the authorities to notify forthwith any person in relation to whom certain contractual decisions are taken. Those decisions are:

   (a) to exclude him from an approved list;

   (b) not to invite him to tender when he had asked to be invited;

   (c) not to accept the submission of his tender;

   (d) not to enter into a contract with him when he has submitted a tender;

   (e) not to approve, or to select or nominate, persons to be sub-contractors for a proposed or subsisting contract; and

   (f) to terminate a contract.

Section 20 also provides that where the person so requests in writing within 15 days of the date of notification, the authority must provide him, within 15 days of the date of the request, with written reasons for the decision.

Transitional Duty Regarding Approved Lists

15.   Section 21 of the Act requires authorities who keep an approved list of contractors to consider whether contractors have been excluded from, or included in, the list by reference to non-commercial matters and, if so, to draw up a new list in accordance with procedures specified in the Act. (It should be noted that Section 22 prevents authorities charging a fee to contractors for inclusion in an approved list.)

16.   The duty to draw up new lists is to be discharged as soon as is reasonably practicable, and in any event by 7 July, 1988.

Financial and Manpower Implications

17.   Overall, the Part II provisions should lead to a reduction in expenditure by those authorities who have constrained competition by introducing non-commercial matters into the contractual process. They should also enable manpower savings to be made by those local authorities who have established contract compliance units.

Enquiries

18.   Enquiries on this circular should be addressed (in England) to LG3 Division, Department of the Environment, 2 Marsham Street, London SW1P 3EB and (in Wales) to WEP Division (LG), Welsh Office, Cathays Park, Cardiff CF1 3NQ.

A H DAVIS, *Assistant Secretary*

A H H JONES, *Assistant Secretary*

The Chief Executive
  County Councils ⎞ in England and Wales
  District Councils ⎠
  London Borough Councils
  Council of the Isles of Scilly
The Town Clerk, City of London
The National Park Officer
  Lake District Special Planning Board
  Peak Park Joint Planning Board

The Chief Executive, Urban Development Corporations
The General Manager, New Town Development Corporations
The Clerk/Secretary Miscellaneous Authorities in England and Wales
[DOE LGR/25/2/01]
[WO LG49/3/47]

LOCAL GOVERNMENT ACT 1988—SECTION 18(5)

Specification of questions and descriptions of evidence

The Secretary of State for the Environment, as respects England, and the Secretary of State for Wales, as respects Wales, in exercise of the powers conferred on them by section 18(5) of the Local Government Act 1988 hereby specify the following questions and description of evidence—

1. Is it your policy as an employer to comply with your statutory obligations under the Race Relations Act 1976 and, accordingly, your practice not to treat one group of people less favourably than others because of their colour, race, nationality or ethnic origin in relation to decisions to recruit, train or promote employees?

2. In the last three years, has any finding of unlawful racial discrimination been made against your organisation by any court or industrial tribunal?

3. In the last three years, has your organisation been the subject of formal investigation by the Commission for Racial Equality on grounds of alleged unlawful discrimination?

If the answer to question 2 is in the affirmative or, in relation to question 3, the Commission made a finding adverse to your organisation,

4. What steps did you take in consequence of that finding?

5. Is your policy on race relations set out—

   (a) in instructions to those concerned with recruitment, training and promotion;

   (b) in documents available to employees, recognised trade unions or other representative groups of employees;

   (c) in recruitment advertisements or other literature?

6. Do you observe as far as possible the Commission for Racial Equality's Code of Practice for Employment, as approved by Parliament in 1983, which gives practical guidance to employers and others on the elimination of racial discrimination and the promotion of equality of opportunity in employment, including the steps that can be taken to encourage members of the ethnic minorities to apply for jobs or take up training opportunities?

Description of evidence

In relation to question 5: examples of the instructions, documents, recruitment advertisements or other literature.

Signed by authority of
the Secretary of State
for the Environment
28 March 1988

A H DAVIS
An Assistant Secretary in the
Department of the Environment

Signed by authority of the
Secretary of State for Wales
28 March 1988

A H H JONES
An Assistant Secretary in the
Welsh Office

Printed in the United Kingdom for Her Majesty's Stationery Office
Dd240101   C58   4/88   GP386   17434

Circular 19/88

Circular from the

Department of the Environment
2 Marsham Street, London SW1P 3EB

8 August 1988

Local Government Act 1988: Part I and Schedule I
Competition in the Provisions of Local Authority Services

1.   I am directed by the Secretary of State for the Environment to refer to Part I and Schedule I of the Local Government Act 1988 ("the Act") which require local authorities and other public bodies, where they wish to carry out certain activities using their own employees, to expose those activities to competition.

2.   This circular is not a detailed resume of Part I of the Act; nor does it purport to offer authoritative interpretations of the Act's provisions. Its aim is to draw to the attention of local authorities certain aspects of the legislation to which the Secretary of State attaches particular importance, and to clarify certain areas where enquiries received suggest that uncertainty exists. In the circular the in-house organisations which carry out work subject to Part I are referred to as Direct Service Organisations or DSOs. Guidance on the other provisions of the Act has already been provided in DOE Circulars 8/88 (which covers Part II of the Act) and 12/88 (which covers Parts III and IV).

Introduction

3.   The purpose of Part I is to improve the efficiency of local authority service provision, and therefore the value for money that local authorities achieve, by requiring fair competition between DSOs and contractors. This will be secured whether the result of the competition is that services remain in-house or are contracted out. The legislation will also mean that authorities will have to set out clearly, in specifications available for inspection by anyone with an interest, precisely what they want to achieve in the services subject to competition. This in itself will yield significant benefits in terms of both accountability and management discipline.

Defined authorities

4.   Section 1 of the Act lists the authorities to which Part I applies ("defined authorities"). These include all tiers of local government—counties, districts and parishes, and a wide range of joint authorities, joint boards, joint committees and other bodies.

Defined activities

5.   Section 2 of the Act lists the activities which authorities will have to expose to competition under the provisions of Part I if they wish to carry them out themselves ("defined activities"). Definitions of the activities are provided in Schedule 1 but authorities may wish to note the points on the individual definitions set out in paragraphs 6-12 below.

6.   **Refuse collection** The Act's definition of refuse collection refers to Section 12 of the Control of Pollution Act 1974, which defines household and commercial waste. The remainder of Section 12 came into force on 6 June

LOCAL GOVERNMENT ACT 1988

Local Government Act 1988 Financial Objectives (England) Specifications 1988

The Secretary of State for the Environment in exercise of the powers conferred on him by section 10(2) of the Local Government Act 1988, and of all other powers enabling him in that behalf, hereby specifies the following:—

PART I

Citation, commencement and interpretation

1.—(1) These specifications may be cited as the Local Government Act 1988 Financial Objectives (England) Specifications 1988 and shall come into operation on 1 September 1988.

(2) In these specifications—

"the Act" means the Local Government Act 1988;

"the account" means, in respect of each defined activity, the account which the defined authority is required to keep under section 9(2) of the Act;

"defined activity" and "defined authority", each have the meanings given to them by the Act;

"financial year" means a period of twelve months beginning in each year on 1 April.

PART II

Scope of Part

2.　This part applies to the defined activities set out in section 2(2)(a) and (c) to (g) of the Act.

Rate of return on capital

3.　A defined authority shall secure, in respect of each financial year in which they carry out a defined activity, that the revenue credited to the account in respect of that activity is sufficient to show a 5% rate of return on any capital employed in carrying out the activity.

Capital employed

4.　Capital is employed in respect of a defined activity if the following conditions are fulfilled:

(a) the invitation to carry out work comprised in a defined activity made under either section 7(4) or section 4(2) or (4) of the Act stated or implied that capital employed should be provided by whoever might be awarded the work, and

(b) the authority owned the capital employed and used it in connection with the carrying out of the work.

Method of calculation of rate of return

5.—(1) The rate of return on the capital employed shall be calculated in accordance with the following formula:

$$\frac{A \times 100}{B}$$

Where 'A' is the current cost operating surplus and 'B' is the value of the capital employed.

11

(2) "Current cost operating surplus" means the difference between:

(a) the revenue credited to the account, and

(b) an amount which is the total of—

(i) an amount equal to the wages, salaries, administration and management expenses incurred,

(ii) an amount equal to the depreciation of fixed assets, plant and machinery based on a value equal to their average current replacement cost,

(iii) the replacement cost of stock used, valued at the time it is used, and

(iv) any other expenditure incurred in, or incidental to, the carrying out of the work, except—

(A) any repayment of sums borrowed (together with interest on any such sum),

(B) any repayment of money (including any payment of interest at the appropriate rate) to a fund from which money has been transferred in accordance with paragraph 19 of Schedule 13 to the Local Government Act 1972 to defray expenditure on a fixed asset, plant or machinery,

(C) any payment to a fund established under paragraph 16 of Schedule 13 to the Local Government Act 1972, and'

(D) expenditure on the acquisition, replacement or major improvement of fixed assets, plant or machinery.

(3) The "value of capital employed" during a financial year shall be determined in accordance with the following formula:

$$\frac{C + D}{2}$$

Where 'C' is the value, on a current cost basis, of the capital employed at the end of the immediately preceding year, and 'D' is the value on a current cost basis of the capital employed at the end of the year in question.

(4) "The value, on a current cost basis, of the capital employed" at the end of a financial year, means the total of—

(a) an amount equal to the current replacement cost of stock or, if there has been a permanent diminution in the value below its current replacement cost, the net realisable value of stock, and

(b) the net current replacement cost of any fixed assets, plant and machinery, being the difference between—

(i) an amount equal to the gross current replacement cost of any fixed assets, plant or machinery; and

(ii) an amount equal to the accumulated depreciation of any fixed asset, plant or machinery calculated on the gross current replacement cost referred to above; or

where there has been a permanent diminution in the value of any such fixed asset, plant or machinery below its net current replacement cost, the net realisable value of that asset.

Chapter Two

The principal players

Many private landscape contractors may well consider that some local authorities are busy playing an alternative game. Existing contractors may fear that authorities are more concerned with protecting their own 'in-house' team than helping outside contractors bid for 'their' work. A look inside a local authority will help.

THE CLIENT

The client side of local authorities are heavily governed by the Local Government Act 1988 and Regulations, as shown in Chapter 1. The Act and Regulations play, perhaps a similar role to that of a referee in a game of football, or the rules in a board game.

Usually, when a new board game is invented, much testing is required to be done. A group of players are locked away for hours to play. In this way, all those little difficulties are detected and eliminated. (Practice makes perfect.)

THE RULES

In many cases, the trials happen when the contracts are up and running. It is a new ball game, both for client and contractor. It has taken many decades for the construction industry to come to agreed conditions; and some would say improvements are still needed.

Furthermore, only when contracts are operational may all the rules come to be fully appreciated. This will occur as disputes arise and the tender documentation is put to the test. Of particular importance will be the interpretation of the documents by different clients and contractors. In cases of disputed interpretations, the correct interpretation will be of interest to the courts as well.

There is one key difference in grounds maintenance contracting compared to the other local authority services (e.g. refuse collection, street cleansing, catering, etc.): a grounds maintenance contract will be let every single year in most areas. Thus the client will have regular opportunity to improve.

Here private sector landscape contractors will be involved in exactly the same ball game as public sector direct works contractors, by law; and moreover, in practice, for both types of organization have their particular strengths and weaknesses.

THE CONTRACTOR'S STRENGTHS AND WEAKNESSES

The strength of the landscape contractor is in the ability to assess and accurately to price jobs of work. It is second nature to an existing contractor. However, the biggest weakness can be in subsequently ensuring sufficient manpower and supervision for the contract.

This will inevitably lead to conflict between the contractor and the client; and this could lead to default procedures and possible termination, unless the faults are rectified to the reasonable satisfaction of the client.

The termination clause of any contract is, perhaps, the most crucial part of any contract document. The time to study this clause is at the tender preparation stage, long before any dispute looms. Of particular importance is the financial penalty which will be incurred if default is proved.

If the contractor defaults, the client may be allowed to bring in a second contractor. If this second contractor costs the client more, then the client may charge the increased cost to the first contractor. Beware, that is a very real penalty.

CONTRACTS AND SIZE

The biggest challenge facing landscape contractors in the future will be to ensure that they are of sufficient size to undertake contracts competently. Contracts will be bigger: the landscape contractor needs to keep the particular strengths of being small and efficient, yet be able to work effectively in a larger organization. There is no room for complacency in the local authority direct works teams.

They have the advantage of knowing intimately the area and the work – they have been doing it for years. But this can easily prove to be their biggest disadvantage. If a local authority wins its own tender, there is a chance that the maintenance teams will carry on just as they have in the past; and if this is without sufficient regard to the written requirements

"If the contract is terminated by the Authority as provided in the Conditions of Contract, then the Authority will be entitled to employ such other persons as it sees fit to carry out the works, using all plant and equipment of the contractor. The Authority will charge all such costs to the contractor. These costs will include the costs incurred by the Authority's officers in making alternative arrangements"

Fig. 2.1 Check particularly the termination clauses

of the contract, they will lose money.

A very real danger of tenders won by the local authority's own contractor is that of any subsequent complacency. All work carried out needs to be only that as specified in writing if a profit is to be made.

An example will illustrate this point. A tarmac contractor quotes to re-surface a driveway, so that is all that he will re-surface. He will not re-surface the garden paths. He must carry out precisely what has been asked of him – and no more. If he were foolish enough to repair footpaths as well, he will simply make a loss. (Soon he would be out of business.)

This example illustrates a simple fact of life. Unfortunately, an existing local authority contractor, all too often, will carry out work which has not been ordered. This is solely due to the fact that the maintenance teams are continuing in their old ways, not as per the printed order or specification. Old habits die hard.

If this work is not claimed for, or not allowed, a loss will be incurred.

Fig. 2.2 Carry out only what is required

COSTING JOBS

A financial loss in future will be as terminal for a public sector direct works organization as for any private company. The other major weakness of direct works teams traditionally is the inability to price jobs. Works are often based on standard minute values, or outdated bonus schemes.

The biggest challenge facing public sector direct works organizations is therefore to work to a quoted price. Simple. But often it will require a fundamental change of attitude.

Work in future will be carried out exactly as stated in the specification. The example given in this chapter is reproduced from the guidelines produced by the Institute of Leisure and Amenity Management (ILAM). The ILAM specifications and draft contract documents are, perhaps, the most comprehensive available; they will be those most likely in use by many authorities.

PROFIT OR LOSS?

Everyone is equal in the eyes of the law. Also, in actual practice, grounds maintenance contractors will be largely governed by the same rules of profit and loss, regardless of whether the contractor is in the public or private sector.

The relatively large size of the tenders on offer may be a significant discouraging factor to many small local landscape companies. In an attempt to help, the Local Government Act 1988 requires authorities to submit grounds maintenance works to tender in at least 20% parcels. This means that a tender may be as small as, say, £100 000 or £200 000.

At the other end of the scale, a 20% tender could be worth £1 million, or more, in a large metropolitan city. That means an awful lot of manpower, equipment and organization.

No doubt, over the years, there will be a metamorphosis. Small companies will grow big – quickly – by takeover or merger or by receiving large commercial investment.

Small companies should not lose heart. Subcontracting will be a feature of many contracts. This will naturally happen due to the great diversity of horticultural works required, and also to the geographical spread of the sites. There should be plenty of opportunity for small companies and for new entrants to start on the ladder.

The most discouraging factor for the direct works organization is the limitation placed on them by law. They can only compete for works inside the public sector. Works in the private sector are taboo: the Local Authorities (Goods and Services) Act 1970 sees to that.

II C-17 Hedge maintenance

17.1 *General*

All hedges are to be pruned to the shape required by the Supervising Officer. This will be one of the preferred shape profiles as defined by the Supervising Officer. The Contractor will at all times provide a stable hedge and must contact the Supervising Officer as soon as possible if he is unable to do so. Hedges must also be impenetrable.

17.2 *Cutting equipment*

(i) The Contractor will use sharp secateurs, shears or mechanical cutters according to the type and location of the hedge; all as stated in the Contract. Correct equipment and attachments must be used.

(ii) All cuts will be clean, and any ragged edges will be removed using a sharp knife, except where side arm flail work is carried out.

17.3 *Method of pruning*

(i) Unless otherwise stated, current growth will be removed back to the old wood, and the hedge will be pruned back to the same height width and general shape as that which existed at the completion of the last approved pruning.

(ii) If the Contractor is provided with plans or working drawings, he will prune the hedge as per the details on these plans or drawings.

(iii) Should the Contractor believe he has been asked to do anything which, in his opinion, is detrimental to the hedge or an obstruction to pedestrians or vehicles, he must notify the Supervising Officer before commencing any work.

17.4 *Highway hedges*

(i) Because of their potentially dangerous location, highway hedges must be cut by the Contractor taking particular account of the following:

a) The Contractor must comply with all Road Traffic Regulations and any other current legislation

b) The Contractor's operatives will wear fluorescent jackets at all times.

c) Unless otherwise stated, work will only be carried out during daylight hours.

d) Traffic lights will be provided by the Contractor.

e) The Contractor will liaise with the Police and the Highway Authority to ensure that all aspects of his work are satisfactory according to law.

Fig. 2.3 ILAM Competitive Tendering (cont.)

17.5　*Tractor-mounted cutting equipment*

(i)　Large, easily accessible highway hedges will be maintained by tractor-mounted cutting equipment (e.g., flail-arm). All machinery must be approved by the Supervising Officer before use and all Road Traffic Regulations must be adhered to, including use of beacons.

17.6　*Times for pruning*

(i)　The Contractor will prune according to the following timetable.

Hedge Species　　　　　　Pruning Period

(Client Note: The Client will have to complete his own timetable, with due regard of geographical location, local topography and sound horticultural practice).

(ii)　Wherever possible the Contractor will avoid the bird-nesting season, generally May and June.

17.7　*Arisings and clippings*

All arisings, including clippings lodged in the hedge, will be cleared from site at the end of each working day and disposed of at a suitable, previously agreed tip. The Contractor may, of course, keep the site clean and tidy and carry out the removal of arisings more frequently than this if he so wishes. All arisings must be removed from the highway.

17.8　*Hedge bases*

(i)　The Contractor will be required to leave the base of the hedge clean, tidy and weedfree on every occasion that the hedge is cut.

(ii)　The Contractor will ensure that his price for hedgecutting quoted in this Contract covers this aspect of work, as no extra costs will be paid to the Contractor for any excess clearing work required to hedge bases, regardless of any extra works necessary.

(iii)　Where hedge bases meet grass, the Contractor must leave this edge neat, vertical and tidy. Specification 10 'Edging' must be read in conjunction with this paragraph. The Contractor will ensure that his rate quoted for hedgecutting in this Contract covers this aspect of work.

(iv)　The width of hedge bases will equal the width of the hedge bottom unless otherwise stated.

17.9　*Special treatment to hedges*

Special treatment may be required by the Supervising Officer (for example, the application of growth retardant) and the Contractor must ensure that he is able to carry out any such instruction within one week of receiving such instruction.

17.10 *Vandalism*
Any vandalised hedge will be reported to the Supervising Officer as soon as possible.

17.11 *Application of pesticides*
(i)   The Contractor will be required to apply an approved pesticide on ... occasions to hedge bases in accordance with the maintenance schedule in this Contract and in accordance with the specification for application of pesticides.

17.12 *Hedge replacement*
The Contractor will be required, on occasion, to replace an existing hedge. Such work will be carried out in accordance with the specification 'Shrubs' C-29, and the rate quoted for shrub planting will apply, together with any appropriate pruning rates. New planting will be supplemented by erection of temporary protective fencing as instructed by the Supervising Officer.

17.13 *Pricing for hedgecutting*
The Contractor will have inspected all hedges specified within this Contract prior to pricing, and the rate quoted will be deemed to include all the aforementioned works.

Furthermore, there are plenty of other restrictions either in Acts of Parliament or in various rules, regulations and codes of conduct.

Never mind, the real world is full of adversities to be overcome. Those in the public sector who have the time to moan about their fate are unlikely to be cut-out for a competitive environment. They would be better advised to address the problems with a positive attitude. It is far more important to find ways to ensure success and overcome any petty restrictions.

Both public and private sector will find themselves on a relatively equal footing. Or to be more accurate, more equal in some respects and less equal in others. At the end of the day, the balance will be there for all to see.

THE CLIENT SIDE

The central control within the authority, is the client. As any business will know, the client is all-important. It is the client who states what is required. The contractor then carries it out: no more, no less. And then the client will pay the sum due, i.e. what the contractor has tendered or quoted.

It is the client side of an authority which will undertake all the preparations for tender, write the specification, decide when and how to seek tenders. All according to the legislation. Little chance of favouritism here.

The client has one overriding requirement: the job well done. However, many clients experience difficulty in stating exactly what work they do want carried out.

KEEPING STANDARDS AND PERFORMANCE

Going out to tender for grounds maintenance has been a new experience for local authorities. The client's starting-point is to keep to current standards of maintenance, at the least. All the client's energies will be directed to that outcome. Any improvements will only come later.

For the client to work via a contractor is obviously going to be very different to undertaking works by directly employed staff. Formality will be increased in a contract situation. It will be increased even further where the client is still wrestling to determine the full range of the works required to be carried out. The effects of poor performance are also increased in a contract situation.

If one employee is guilty of poor performance, that employee can be disciplined or dismissed. This has only a small effect on the total maintenance work. Dismiss a contractor and the effect on the maintenance work is total.

Maintenance ceases.

The client therefore needs to establish with some certainty that a contractor, if chosen, will be able to perform.

SELECTION

Thus the evaluation of **tenderers** is just as important as the subsequent evaluation of **tenders**. In preparing a tender, the client will place much emphasis on gaining sufficient information about every person or company interested in tendering. The client will be looking for much more than a good impression.

This explains all the questioning of tenderers that is required before being allowed to fill in a tender.

Clients are well practised in preparing select lists of contractors for specific contracts. Only those contractors selected by the client are ever invited to submit tenders.

Contractor selection and viability

Clients will invariably seek to reduce the number of contractors applying to a selected few. Private sector landscape contractors can rest assured that this is not a back-door method of excluding them. At least three private sector contractors must be included in a select list (given, of course, that at least three apply). It is the rules again.

Advertisements will invite persons interested in tendering to submit details of themselves. Those expressing an interest will then be the subject of some considerable scrutiny by the client.

The client's foremost task will be to select contractors who could adequately perform the contract – if it were awarded to them. Two key elements of the selection will include:

- *Technical ability* e.g. has the contractor sufficient experience of similar contracts in the past? Is he or she knowledgeable about horticulture, play equipment, groundsmanship, greenkeeping and all the other specialisms needed to run the contract competently?
- *Financial ability* e.g. has the contractor sufficient financial resources to incur the necessary expenditure for machinery, vehicles and plant? Also the necessary call on cash reserves to pay wages and all the other costs incurred in the performance of the contract, especially in that initial gap prior to being paid by the client?

A thorough appraisal will be undertaken by most clients, especially in grounds maintenance. This is due to this type of maintenance work not having been traditionally the subject of tendering in the past. Clients will be wary.

All contractors should therefore ensure that they make the best account of themselves.

Critical analysis

The client will be just as critical of the in-house, contractor as outside contractors. Not only do the regulations demand this, but the client will be aware that both types of organization have their weaknesses.

That level of scrutiny, prior to even having a chance of filling in the tender documents, may seem unfair. This is especially true of those who are just setting up in business.

That is why it is so important to understand fully the client's viewpoint. A successful contractor will understand (and bear with) the hesitation incurred during the scrunity process.

The complexity of a grounds maintenance contract has been known to defeat the most able of contractors.

The client will need to scrutinize thoroughly at least three applicants from the private sector, together with any in-house bid. He will need to be fully satisfied that each tenderer does indeed have the necessary competence and capacity.

Fig. 2.4   The contractor needs to give more than just a good impression

Once the best three or four (or more) contractors have been selected, price will then have a large influence on the allocation of the contract.

Subcontracting

Of particular interest to newly established contractors is the fact that approved subcontractors will be a feature of many successful contracts. This will also be of interest to specialist contractors, who will often be able to find their niche in the market-place.

For any new landscape contractor or small specialist contractor (e.g. a company specializing in chemical weedkilling or play equipment maintenance), it is vitally important to achieve early publicity.

Many main contractors setting out to win the total tender will seek prices from subcontractors. For them to be successful, they will need to know beforehand competent subcontractors and their prices. When submitting a tender, a main contractor will not have the time for seeking subcontractors; he needs that information long before.

There will be but one winner per contract. Obviously, there will be a greater number of disillusioned losers. As in any race, the best man wins. However, it may be of some comfort to losers to ask the winner how many times he has previously failed. The answer should be obvious. Winners are bred by inching a bit nearer to their goal each time.

The whole tendering process undertaken by the client is governed by regulations. Many of the detailed rules are provided by government, other regulations and Codes of Conduct are published and made available by professional bodies and organizations.

Students of red tape will have a field day.

For those with a business to operate, there is no better advice than to start applying for invitations now.

The reason for failure

Many who apply for selection will fail. However, the Codes of Conduct will form the basis of the evaluation. Contractors who fail should ask the client why. There will always be a reason. The opportunity should be taken by contractors to press home their own advantages, despite the fact they have failed. Being known is half the battle. They should not miss an opportunity to mention that they are available (even as a subcontractor). It can only help their subsequent chances.

Furthermore, not every contract lasts for the stipulated three to six years. Disputes and disagreements lead to a proportion being terminated. In this situation, a client needs to know of good local contractors who can step in at short notice.

It should be possible to see the price of the winning tender, also the names of those who submitted bids. Although it may not be possible to determine which company has submitted what bid, the key factors of financial offer and company names should be known. The rules have been drawn up with the intention of trying to ensure fair competition and the release of key information. In that way, everyone will be better informed for future tender submissions. Some will be surprised by the results.

The highest tender is sometimes twice that of the lowest.

For every successful bid, there may well be at least three or four unsuccessful ones – and even more unsuccessful applicants. For those who are unsuccessful, it is still worth keeping a close interest.

The information gleaned about the winning bids is of great importance. The client should provide the information which is to be made public (price and companies tendering). In addition, essential details will be found in the local authority's minutes in the public library.

For the contractor who succeeds in his tender: excellent; but the hard work starts now. That is the subject of the next chapter.

SUMMARY

Before that work is addressed, we should summarize here the main aspects covered in this chapter:

- Grounds maintenance by tender is something new for almost everyone.
- The rules of the new game can be learnt by reading the Local Government Act 1988, reading the tender documents of a nearby local authority, applying for invitations to tender and by completing tenders.
- Experience is always a good teacher. Many will watch how the tenders are won and operated over the years.
- Public sector and private sector contractors are treated the same. They have to be, as per the rules of the game and overseen by central government.
- Both public and private sector contractors have their strengths and weaknesses.
- A contractor who knows his own strengths and weaknesses (and those of his competitors) is in a strong position.
- Rules and regulations are there to ensure fair competition.
- The contractor side of a local authority is separate from the client side.
- The client side is boss.
- The client will only seek tenders from persons or companies who can deliver subsequently.

- The financial and technical capacity of a contractor will be fundamental in being selected to tender.
- The total tender price is critically important in determining the winning bid.
- All contractors, both big and small and public and private, should never miss a chance to make themselves known to clients.

Attached to this chapter is an example of an appraisal process for tenderers. This particular appraisal is part of the tender documents published by the Institute of Leisure and Amenity Management, and will no doubt be used by many authorities.

Only competent contractors need apply . . .

The importance of the appraisal is simple. It is a method to try to select competent contractors. Authorities will be seeking contractors with a proven track record of performance in the particular kind of work together with adequate financial backing. In other words, contractors who will be available to perform if appointed. Only when selected will these contractors be invited to submit tender prices for the works proposed.

Having said all that, all contracts operate on a basis of mutual confidence. Every opportunity should be taken to increase confidence. In addition to any formal appraisal, interviews are of great value – so are site visits.

ADDENDUM: APPRAISAL OF TENDERERS

Reproduced with kind permission of the Institute of Leisure and Amenity Management from: *Competitive Tendering: Maintenance of Grounds and Open Spaces*, (Longman, 1988).

This addendum emphasises the importance which Authority will place on selecting only competent contractors.

The questionnaires supplied by clients delve into all aspects of a contractor, in a bid to select only competent contractors for the shortlist. This type of questionnaire should be welcomed by most proficient contractors.

The completed questionnaires will soon eliminate any cowboy contractors. Furthermore, it will save the time and effort of many contractors in pursuing a tender submission where the size and type of a particular contract is unsuitable.

I(B): Sample tenderer appraisal questionnaire

TENDERER APPRAISAL FORM
[(19   )]
FOR GROUNDS MAINTENANCE

<u>Please answer all questions</u>

Trading name of Contractor: . . . .

Full name of Contractor: . . . .

Address of Registered Office: . . . .

                                            . . . .

                                            . . . .

                                            . . . .

Telephone number: . . . .

Registration number: . . . .

Address and telephone number   . . . .
of office from where business is
conducted, if different from   . . . .
above:
                                            . . . .

                                            . . . .

Name of person applying on   . . . .
behalf of the Contractor:
                                            . . . .

Position in company: . . . .

General and Technical Details

Office
Use
Only

1. Please complete the following table in respect of value of work for which invitations to tender are sought.

*Denote Value	a	b	c	d	e
1. Grounds Maintenance					

*NOTE: Indicate contract values by ticking appropriate squares

(a) Contracts up to £25 000
(b) Contracts up to £25 000–£100 000
(c) Contracts up to £100 000–£250 000
(d) Contracts up to £250 000–£600 000
(e) Over £600 000 — state amount £....................

2. Please state below the full names of any technical associations, employers, or trade associations or guarantee schemes of which your Company is a member. Where appropriate, please indicate the maximum value of any one contract covered by the guarantee scheme.

Full name of Organisation	Registration Membership No. (if any)	Value of work guaranteed	Date of membership expiration

continued

3. <u>Surety:</u> In the event of your Company being awarded a contract, you would be required to provide a performance bond of ....% of the tender sum — please confirm that you would be prepared to do this.

. . . .

. . . .

. . . .

. . . .

. . . .

4. Do you undertake any form of contract maintenance besides horticulture? If so, please give details

5. Please list the addresses of any workshops or premises/depots which you would use when working for .... Council

Financial information

WHERE A SOLE TRADER OR PARTNERSHIP

6. Please state full name(s) of proprietor and every partner.

7. Please state date of formation.

continued

Office Use Only

WHERE A LIMITED COMPANY

Office Use Only

8. Please state whether the Company is public or private.

9. Please state full names of every director or partner, manager or secretary.

10. Please state date of registration and the registration number under the Companies Act, 1948–1981.

    or

11. Please state date of registration and the registration number under the Industrial and Provident Societies Acts, 1965–1968.

12. If a limited company, please state nominal and paid up capital.

13. Please confirm that the objects of the company, as set out in memorandum of association, cover purposes for which this list is being compiled. A copy of the memorandum of association should be returned along with this form

14. Please list wholly owned subsidiary companies (attach separate sheet if necessary).

continued

14.a If your company is a subsidiary of a member of a group of companies, or other group members please name the parent company and/or other group members.

14.b If your company is a subsidiary of any other company confirmation is required that the holding company will be prepared to issue a guarantee in respect of any contract which may be awarded to the company applying.

Parent company prepared to issue a guarantee.

Yes	No

(Delete as appropriate)

15. Have any claims/litigation ever been successfully made against your Company? If so give details.

15.a Please give details of any outstanding claims or litigation against your Company and/or your ultimate holding company.

16. Please state name and address of bankers for reference.

17. Please state annual turnover for the last five years.

Dates	Turnover	% due to Grounds Maintenance
1983–4		
1984–5		
1985–6		
1986–7		
1987–8		

17.a Please state your VAT registration number.

continued

18.a Please provide the following information on your employer's liability insurance.			Office Use Only

18.a Please provide the following information on your employer's liability insurance.	**Limit of Cover**	£	
	Insurer		
	Policy Number		
	Expiry Date		

19. Please provide the following information on your public liability insurance.	**Limit of Cover**	£	
	Insurer		
	Policy Number		
	Expiry Date		

If your public and employers liability insurance cover is for less than £5m., please confirm that you would be prepared to make cover of this amount available in the event of your being awarded a contract.

Yes	**No**

(Delete as appropriate)

20. Have any of your directors/partners/proprietors or other employees ever been employed by this Authority?

Yes	**No**

(Delete as appropriate)

21. If the answer to the above is yes, please give the name of the person employed, the capacity in which they were employed and the dates of their employment.

continued

Required documents

22. Please enclose a full set of audited accounts for each of the last three years.

Enclosed	Yes	No

(Delete as appropriate)

23. Please provide a copy of the Certificate of Incorporation of your Company under Section 13 of the Companies Act 1948 (if applicable).

24. If your Company holds a Tax Exemption Certificate under the Construction Industry Tax Deduction Scheme, please enclose a copy.

Enclosed	Yes	No

(Delete as appropriate)

25. Does your Company hold a certifying document in a line with the provisions of the Finance (No. 2) Act 1975, stating:

Yes	No

(Delete as appropriate)

   a) the type of certificate held
   b) the certificate number
   c) the name in which the certificate was issued
   d) address of the issuing office.

26. If your answer to the previous question was yes, please enclose a copy of the certifying document.

Health and safety at work

27. Please state what if any arrangements are made by your organisation to ensure your employees carry out their obligations under the Health and Safety at Work Act 1974.

Details of workforce: directly employed

28. Please state the total number of personnel regularly employed.

Category	Number Employed
Total Staff	
Tradespeople	
Trainees/ Apprentices	
Off-Site Management	
On-Site Management Supervision	
General Office/Admin Staff	

29. Please provide a copy of your management structure showing the supervision of your workforce.

Enclosed	Yes	No

(Delete as appropriate)

30. Please provide details of qualifications of your company's directly employed workforce below

Trade	Workforce Excluding Those Under Training			
	Minimum Recognised Qualifications of staff	Supervisors Foreman/ Chargehand	Operatives	Total
Maintenance of fine turf	No. holding C & G Phase II Groundsmanship			
Maintenance of sportsfields	No. holding C & G Phase II Groundsmanship			
Pruning of shrubs, roses	No. holding C & G phase II horticulture			
Application of pesticides	No. holding certificate of competence			
Driving	No. holding full licence			
Driving HGV	No. holding HGV licence			
Driving PSV	No. holding PSV licence			
Use of tractor mounted flail arm	5 years' experience			
Use of chainsaws	Registered user			
Number of Qualified Firstaiders	Recognised Course of Training			

31. Please provide an estimate of the qualifications of your company's directly employed workforce that could be made available on site for proposed contract.

Office Use Only

| Trade | Estimate of workforce that could be made available for this contract | | | |
	Minimum Required Qualifications of staff	Supervisors Foreman/ Chargehand	Operatives	Total
Maintenance of fine turf	C & G Phase II Groundsmanship			
Maintenance of sportsfields	C & G Phase II Groundsmanship			
Pruning of shrubs, roses	C & G phase II horticulture			
Application of pesticides	Certificate of competence			
Driving	Full licence			
Driving HGV	HGV licence			
Driving PSV	PSV licence			
Use of tractor mounted flail arm	5 years' experience			
Use of chainsaws	Registered user			
Tree Climbing	Recognised course of training			
Number of Qualified Firstaiders	Recognised Course of Training			

continued

32. Please state the estimated number of off-site management that could be made available for proposed Contract.

Number	

33. Is it your policy as an employer to comply with your statutory obligations under the Race Relations Act 1976 and, accordingly, your practice not to treat one group of people less favourably than others because of their colour, race, nationality or ethnic origin in relation to decisions to recruit, train or promote employees.

Yes	**No**

(Delete as appropriate)

34. In the last three years, has any finding of unlawful racial discrimination been made against your organisation by any court or industrial tribunal?

Yes	**No**

(Delete as appropriate)

35. In the last three years, has your organisation been the subject of formal investigation by the Commission for Racial Equality on grounds of alleged unlawful discrimination?

Yes	**No**

(Delete as appropriate)

36. If the answer to question 34 is in the affirmative or, in relation to question 35, the Commission made a finding adverse to your organisation, what steps did you take in consequence of that finding?

. . . .

. . . .

. . . .

. . . .

continued

37. Is your policy on race relations set out:-

Office
Use
Only

a) in instructions to those concerned with recruitment, training and promotion:

Yes	No

(Delete as appropriate)

b) in documents available to employees, recognised trade unions or other representative groups of employees:

Yes	No

(Delete as appropriate)

c) in recruitment advertisements or other literature?

Yes	No

(Delete as appropriate)

Please provide examples of any such documents, instructions, rec. adverts or other such literature.

38. Do you observe as far as possible the Commission for Racial Equality's Code of Practice for Employment, as approved by Parliament in 1983, which gives practical guidance to employers and others on the elimination of racial discrimination and the promotion of equality of opportunity in employment, including the steps that can be taken to encourage members of the ethnic minorities to apply for jobs or take up training opportunities?

(Delete as appropriate)

Yes	No

Compliance with the Council's Standing Orders

Client Note: Amend accordingly.
39. The Council's Standing Order no. 15 states that:

There shall be inserted in every written contract, a clause empowering the Council to cancel the contract and to recover from the contractor the amount of any loss resulting from such cancellation, if the contractors shall have offered or given or agreed to give to any person any gift or consideration of any kind as an inducement or reward for doing or forbearing to do   continued or having done or forborne to do any action in relation to the obtaining or execution of the contract or any other contract with the Council, or for showing or forbearing to show favour or disfavour to any person in relation to the contract or any other contract with the Council, or if the like acts shall have been done by any person employed by them or acting on their behalf (whether with or without the knowledge of the contractors) or if in relation to any contract with the Council the contractors or any person employed by them or acting on their behalf shall have committed any offence under the Prevention of Corruption Acts, 1889–1916, or any amendment or re-enactment thereof; or shall have given any fee or reward the receipt of which is an offence under sub-section (2) of Section 117 of the Local Government Act 1972.

40. Please indicate that you understand the implications of the standing order and that you will comply with it.

Yes	No

(Delete as appropriate)

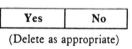

Details of workload

41. Please list on Schedule 'A' overleaf all Grounds Maintenance Contracts currently being carried out as well as all of those that have been completed within the last three years. Do you agree that we may approach any or all of the clients listed without further reference to you.

Yes	No

(Delete as appropriate)

Schedule 'A': Details of workload

(To be completed further to question 41)

PROJECT DETAILS				EMPLOYER	SUPERVISING OFFICER/PERSON TO WHOM REFERENCE CAN BE MADE		
Project Title	Value £000s	Start Date	Completion Date		Name	Address	Tel. No.

When you have completed the questionnaire, please read and sign the section below

I/We certify that the information supplied is accurate to the best of my/our knowledge and that I/We accept the conditions and undertakings requested in the questionnaire. I/We understand that false information could result in my/our exclusion from the approved list of contractors.

I/We also understand that is is a criminal offence, punishable by imprisonment, to give or offer any gift, or to offer any gift or consideration whatsoever as an inducement or reward to any servant or a Public Body and that any such action will empower the Council to cancel my contract currently in force and will result in my/our exclusion from the approved list of contractors.

Please note that the term 'Contractor' refers to: sole proprietor, partnership, incorporated company or co-operative etc. as appropriate. The undertaking should be signed by the applicant, a partner or authorised representative in his/her own name and on behalf of the Company.

Signed . . . . For and on behalf of . . . .

. . . .

Name . . . . Date . . . .
(in block capitals)

Chapter Three

Preparing to tender

Preparing to submit a competitive tender is a big step for any contractor, no matter how big or small.

COMPARATIVE ADVANTAGES AND FRUSTRATIONS

There tends to be a feeling of 'the grass is greener. . .': small landscape contractors often believe that only the larger companies can compete successfully, due to the complexity of the documentation. Likewise, some larger contractors are aware of the benefits which the small local contractor enjoys. This shows itself in the ability of the local contractor to be able to deliver, once a contract is let.

Some authorities will advise a contractor when they consider that the tender is too big for his capabilities. This, then, can save the contractor time and trouble in preparing a tender submission, while allowing more profitable use of his time on a size of contract to which he is more suited.

In most areas of the country, with many contracts being let on an annual basis, there will continue to be widespread interest shown by a range of landscape contractors. That interest will increase as the practice and methods of tendering become more familiar. Educationalists call it the 'learning curve'.

The process may be likened to climbing a steep mountain carrying a heavy backpack. The weight of documents tends to deaden the enthusiasm of even the keenest. Invariably (for the climber) peak after peak appears out of the mist before the summit is reached. Similarly with the tendering process, there will often seem yet another stage to undergo, before the competition is finished. The first mountain that anybody ever attempts to climb must appear awesome, yet reaching the summit is exhilarating, however exhausting. Of course, competitive tendering is unlikely to match those extreme emotions, but the analogy is valid.

Tenders vary...

A brief outline model tender is given in Appendix A at the end of this book. This provides a clear guideline to the type of make-up to be seen in tenders. However, tenders greatly differ from one another. This reflects the very varied types of work in each authority's area. And it also reflects the client's desire for close, or loose, controls.

Similarly, landscape contractors vary in size and strength, in fact no two are ever alike. Each has built up over time its own particular strengths. Often these strengths will lie in highly specific areas, like hard or soft landscape works, ornamental horticulture, fencing or arboriculture.

...so do contractors

Contractors necessarily attune themselves to the requirements of the local market. Sometimes this development of particular specialisms is not the result of a conscious decision. A contractor often changes the services he provides by meeting new demands.

Evolving, changing gradually by degrees, is impossible with competitive tendering, rather it is a quantum leap. This is perhaps the real reason for the difficulty experienced by so many. Gradual change over many years can be relatively easily accommodated by companies and organizations. Changes take place almost imperceptibly. With competitive tendering, the change is sudden and dramatic. The sheer size of the task is testimony to that.

There is only one way to prepare for change of this magnitude. The

Fig. 3.1 Ask plenty of questions

way to succeed is to become more and more immersed in the new environment: read plenty of tender documents; apply for inclusion on potential client lists of 'contractors to be invited to tender'; and attend plenty of meetings and site visits provided by clients. Determined contractors never hesitate to ask questions, to familiarize themselves with the situation.

TONY ULYETT'S EXPERIENCE

One such landscape contractor is Tony Ulyett, whose business is in Nottinghamshire. Seeing the new order taking shape in public authority grounds maintenance, he determined to make himself and his company better known. Furthermore, he made a positive attempt to scale the heights, to take on the authorities on their own terms.

'I have had considerable experience of this type of work with some local authorities,' he explained, 'but never before on such a large scale. Nevertheless, I responded to a number of public advertisements. I gained very valuable knowledge.' Tony found that most clients tried to be helpful. They explained much of the background detail necessary to submit a tender. One particular contract to interest him was for the grounds maintenance work in a large public park, which included various sports facilities.

It was a distinct area of maintenance which he could easily envisage managing with his existing methods of working. It was also within easy reach of his work base. Although he was not successful in winning that tender bid, he believes that he was treated fairly and that the experience was entirely worthwhile.

However, at least one authority proved most difficult and obstructive. 'To a certain extent, it depends on the actual client officer with whom you are dealing,' he says, and adds:

> One made it quite clear that he did not want the competition; he did not want private contractors; and he did not want others interfering in what he regarded as his patch. In general, though, I was treated fairly by most authorities. The biggest difficulty to overcome was the variety of work. I had not foreseen the need to provide a 24-hour operation. Nor had I expected the work to include the cleaning of changing-rooms and toilets, or the digging of graves. I had no relevant experience.

Tony Ulyett emphasized the difficulty of dealing with those items of work which lay outside traditional grounds maintenance. As a land scape contractor of many years' standing, he was not prepared or equipped to manage the so-called 'leisure management' aspects of the contract.

Although Tony entered for a number of tenders, he was not successful. But he has no regrets, and he feels he is much more experienced than before he started. He hopes to be able to submit further tenders in future, perhaps with a little more confidence. It is a case of 'try, try and try again' – eventually, he will succeed. Tony will also more easily find the type of contract that interests him, and more particularly, the type of contract in which he can be competitive.

Tony Ulyett also found that all the interviews with client officers were tough – very interesting, very valuable but also very searching. However, he believes that he used those opportunties to learn as much about the client as they learned about him. The interviews also helped to make the appraisal of tender documentation less daunting.

Most companies start from small beginnings and grow over the years. Their size is a definite indication of their success in a highly competitive area. However, some companies lately have started big. The 1988 Act has also led to a number of management buy-outs.

But invariably 'management buy-out' is the wrong term. Although the management is involved, the buy-out aspect of the deal is often minimal. Nevertheless, it is a widely used term and generally understood to mean the transfer of responsibility from an existing employer to the employees.

PARKFIELD LANDSCAPES

Such a process led to the birth of Parkfield Landscapes. This contractor had previously constituted the directly employed workforce of North Avon District Council, near Bristol. 'It was not seen as a way to avoid the implications of the Act', explained Richard Foinette, the Managing Director:

> The idea came about due to the immense workload involved for the Council in preparing for compulsory competitive tendering. A workload and a cost which was seen to be particularly onerous for a relatively small local authority. And time was not on the side of the Council.

The Local Government Act 1988, in effect, does not allow a public authority to carry out grounds maintenance by directly employed staff, unless that work has been won fairly in competition with private sector contractors.

Indeed, the opposite to that is bound to follow. Thus if a public authority does not carry out works using directly employed staff, there is no need to be saddled with the enormous disruption of preparing for grounds maintenance by competitive tender. This obvious (but frequently overlooked) aspect of the 1988 Act was recognized by North Avon District Council, for the value it could bring.

This arrangement has bought time,' Richard Foinette continued:

A four-and-a-half-year contract period was agreed between the Council and Parkfield Landscapes, to continue the grounds maintenance as previously. It has substantial benefits for everyone concerned, including the local residents, who will continue to enjoy the same standards of service at substantial saving.

The amount of tender documentation necessary for grounds maintenance was known to be enormous if the subsequent contract was to be effective. Preparing the maps and measurements alone was seen to be a mammoth task, and costly in itself. In addition, it was seemingly unnecessary when a competent workforce was already employed – one who knew the work area in every detail. The same applied to the type and standard of work.

'Ground maintenance is very different, much more variable than, say, refuse collection.' Richard stated: 'It is easier to monitor and check refuse collection: either the bins have been emptied or they haven't – the evidence is for all to see.'

Grounds maintenance is much different. Take a bowling-green as an example. Once the groundsman has finished cutting the green, it is almost impossible to see whether it has been cut that morning or the previous day, except to the most experienced eye. Moreover, even if that experienced eye were available the same morning, it would be an almost impossible matter to prove in a dispute. North Avon Council had certainly spent some time thinking this one out.

The council was not spared the formalities. The proposal had to be checked and double-checked by the government and the District Auditor. As Parkfield Landscapes were one of the leaders, there were no government guidelines prepared. The auditors had to satisfy themselves that all was as it appeared to be. For example, the assets were acquired on the basis of independent valuation.

In particular, the council could demonstrate real cost savings; in a tight financial climate that would be welcomed by any organization, either public or private. The council escaped from any possible redundancy payments, either now or in the future; and further significant savings were achieved by not having to produce all the specifications and tender documents in such a short space of time. It also greatly reduced the uncertainty which the council faced.

Of course, the other half of the equation is the workforce. And any bargain or agreement needs the willing consent of both parties. Richard Foinette explained:

> That was achieved by a simple majority vote, taken amongst all the staff concerned. With grounds maintenance there was an almost unanimous vote to go our own way. Some other sections voted to stay with the council – and so they did. There was no compulsion.

In this manner, the existing workforce retained their jobs and the council was assured about the standard of service in the coming four years. A lump-sum contract was awarded, based on maintaining existing standards. A Schedule of Rates was prepared and a detailed specification, together with Bills of Quantity, followed later.

An outsider might argue that an agreement such as this is open to abuse. Perhaps the standards would not be reached. Well, that has to be accepted as a real possibility, but surely this is equally possible with all legal agreements and contracts? In day-to-day reality it is necessary to rely entirely on trust and confidence. Parkfield Landscape extended this trust and confidence to the day-to-day operation within the contractor organization:

> We had an outdated bonus system before, which we simply merged with the basic wage. This then allowed us to concentrate on profit-sharing as the real incentive. And, of course, profit is totally linked to productivity. Our working hours had to change as well.

Fig. 3.2   Profit-sharing is linked to productivity

Now, we work variable hours according to the season and the workload.

Like any other business, Parkfield Landscapes is looking for new business ventures. No matter how secure the base provided by the council contract, there are definite limitations to the quantity of business to be expected from that quarter. And just as the quantity is limited, so is the variety of work it provides.

In signing the agreement with the council, the new contractor had to accept various legal and planning restrictions on his activities. For example, the municipal nursery had to be used for plant production only for the council. In addition to the planning control, there was a restrictive covenant in the lease.

So Parkfield Landscapes had to look outside their immediate area for work. In particular, there were some large new housing developments under way within easy reach of their base. Close liaison with the Landscape Architect responsible for the development proved valuable.

There are other local authorities to work for too.

SOURCES OF WORK AND MANAGEMENT BUY-OUTS

Authorities, as variable in size as the county council and the local parish council are all valuable sources of work. Tree planting schemes, in particular, provide extensive work at a time of year when work is most needed – that is the winter. There is always a variety of other work, if sought. Discussions with nearby councils will often prove fruitful.

Nearly everyone who has taken part in a management buy-out (or co-operative venture, or other form of changed ownership) speaks of the months of agony involved. On top of all the hard work of preparing the priced bid, there is the burdensome uncertainty. (Uncertainty, mixed with the real fears about the ability to go it alone – for better or worse).

Management buy-outs do not form part of an exact science. Each is governed by its own particular circumstances, and by the personalities involved. However, one feature common to all buy-outs is the feeling of journeying into the unknown, the unexpected.

At last, when every eventuality seems to have been anticipated and planned for, an unexpected commotion can occur. Then there are so many features which need to be arranged: capital finance, insurance cover, and financial bonds and guarantees. All this when, as yet, the company has no established credibility in financial circles, due to its lack of a proven track record. Combined with these problems are the hopes and aspirations of each individual – soaring high one day, foundering on the rocks the next.

Bureaucratic hurdles abound which can obstruct a personal desire to get back to grass roots, to serve the customer, the community charge payer or sports player better than before. Perhaps, for the first time, bureaucracy is identified as being everywhere, not just in the local town hall. Unfortunately, a city banker can take just as long to deliberate on a matter as a local government committee.

Personal emotions and financial plans are intermixed when an individual has the option of putting his own hard-won savings into the venture. But there is no better way of promoting total commitment. From the part-time clerk to the managing director, all should contribute. Indeed, all do contribute to the success of the venture via their working capacity. Therefore all the more reason why that contribution should be matched in financial terms.

A betting man believes that money has to be placed on a horse for there to be any real interest in the race. An athlete believes that total commitment is essential to even stand a chance in a race, let alone of winning. Competitive tendering is no different. There is a tidal pull towards management buy-outs, as each organization starts to prepare for its own submission for tendering.

STAYING IN HOUSE

There is a lot to be said for staying within an authority. However, those authorities who have set up their own competitive direct work organizations tend to find that they take up a stand-off position, even if they do not go to the extent of becoming a formally separate company.

Whether an in-house bid is made from within an authority, or whether a bid is made during the transition to becoming a separate company, the workload and emotion remain. Everyone involved in a buy-out situation refers to an intensely personal experience. Each individual has to decide his own destiny, to decide to what extent he wishes to commit himself to the future organization. It is far more momentous than achieving success in, say, a job interview. A buy-out raises questions about the very basics of career development, long-term job prospects and alternative life-options.

REWARDS AND SATISFACTION

At the end of the day, the financial implications and potential rewards are not of paramount importance – it is a safe prediction that there will be very few self-made millionaires from ground maintenance contracts.

But there will be thousands and tens of thousands whose livelihood will depend on amenity horticulture and ground maintenance.

Most people working in ground maintenance, in whatever capacity, do so because they have an affinity with the land and its vegetation. Computers and sophisticated management techniques make no impact on the four seasons. Nor can they affect the cyclical rhythms of growth and decay. It is the challenge and satisfaction of managing the land and its vegetation which is the greatest motivation for those involved in horticulture. Horticulture has always been a home for individuals, a place where each person knows and sees his own contribution and achievements.

Being able to manage a task with the minimum of overhead control is a strong and attractive stimulus. More than anything else, it is that combination of increased personal control linked with a career in ground maintenance which motivates most people who participate in a buy-out.

Horticulture tends to be a career for life: generally a mid-career change of major proportions is unwelcome. So, maintenance of the status quo must be a better option for existing employees. If linked to a service, and more important, to payment for that service, then everyone must benefit.

A buy-out may also help local residents. Those standards which the public has come to expect will continue. All those odd little bits of green space tucked away in remote corners will continue to be mown; and sportsmen can reasonably expect to enjoy the same standard of pitch or green preparation.

SUMMARY

Here is a summary of the essential points made in this chapter, including points from the landscape contractors quoted:

- Preparing to submit a tender can be a daunting task.
- It can be likened to climbing a mountain with a heavy pack.
- The summit seems always yet another few hundred feet away.
- All tenders vary – so do contractors.
- The easiest way to learn is to submit applications to local public authorities, and discuss tenders with potential clients.
- Clients vary too: some encourage, some discourage.
- The Nottinghamshire landscape contractor, Tony Ulyett, was unsuccessful with the bids he made. But he is now well placed for future applications.
- He found personal contact very helpful in making the tender documents more meaningful.

- Some landscape contracting companies have been formed, following a buy-out (or similar) from a public authority.
- Parkfield Landscapes, near Bristol, is one such company.
- Where this happens, there are benefits both to employees and employer.
- As long as there remains the same standard of service to the public, in a proven cost-effective manner, then everyone should gain.
- The grounds maintenance personnel of North Avon District Council were confident that their experience and competence made a buy-out a viable option.
- The Distrcit Council was thus saved much cost and uncertainty, yet it had to be satisfied that this would prove financially beneficial.
- And so did the government and its agencies.
- There were very real institutional difficulties to be overcome in transferring to a separate company.
- Setting up the new company was not without a measure of personal trauma.
- Each individual had to decide where his own future lay, then vote accordingly.
- Working methods, working hours and pay structures had to change to be more closely geared to the workload.
- Being a separate, private company allows expansion into other areas of work such as the landscape works associated with a new private housing development.
- This type of work was previously denied, by law.
- Management buy-outs tend to concentrate the mind.
- No one will become a millionaire; that is not what it is all about.
- However, a successful buy-out protects jobs and allows continuity in a chosen career path.
- A new company needs initial capital for machinery, equipment and wages for the first few months.
- The amount of financial commitment made by the personnel has a great influence on the attitude of banks and credit companies.
- Being involved in a buy-out is emotionally demanding, even draining.
- For success, those involved must believe implicitly in their ability to do the job better than anyone else.
- They then must do just that!

The two landscape contractors mentioned in this chapter are very different; but both have seen the new order coming about and responded in the best way they know.

There is no single ideal solution to the competitive tendering situation, just as there is no one ideal tender. Circumstances differ up and down the country. Every contractor (public or private) is his own best adviser on how to go about tendering in his own locality – may the best tenderer win!

ADDENDUM: CHECK-LIST FOR TENDER SUBMISSION

1. Check all local papers weekly for adverts.
2. Check the national, horticultural and municipal journals which are published weekly.
3. When an advert appears, telephone the client named and arrange an appointment.
4. Do not be dissuaded by size, or complexity. Listen and learn.
5. Read the tender documents in the local authority's office; there will be no charge.
6. Check the bank for a financial reference.
7. Check technical references. A potential client will set great store by past clients.
8. If a serious bid is being considered, talk to the client again. Build up mutual confidence.
9. Purchase a copy of the tender document.
10. Submit a request to be invited to tender. Submit it early.
11. If not invited to submit a tender, ask why.
12. If invited to submit a tender, the hard work now begins.
13. Undertake all necessary estimates, and price the document. Discuss prices with everyone, especially the teams who will be carrying out the work, and trade union representatives.
14. Make all the necessary formal arrangements with: (a) solicitor; (b) bank; (c) trade unions; and (d) accountant.
15. Submit the tender on time – not one minute late. Use the plain envelope provided, with no indication of the tenderer's identity.

Chapter Four

Specifications and plants

INSTRUCTIONS, AGREEMENT AND CONFIDENCE

The basis of any good contract is agreement. Next to agreement comes mutual confidence.

Neither agreement nor confidence are possible where there is a lack of clearly understood objectives. And there is only one way to ensure that objectives and goals are clear and explicit – namely, by the written word. Furthermore the written word needs to be concise; and leave no room for doubt as to its exact meaning.

'Cut the bowling-green' may be an adequate instruction from a supervisor to an experienced greenkeeper. As an instruction in a tender document it is worthless.

Any contractor should question loose wording.

Unless every single task is clearly defined; there can be no measure of quality or agreement. 'Cut the bowling-green' could result in an unscrupulous contractor using a rotary mower to cut the bowling-green, or a pair of scissors to cut just one corner.

Full details are crucial.

Any competent contractor will price for the least-cost method of achieving the written word.

If the contract does not say that the bowling-green needs to be cut before 10 a.m., there is presumably no need to price for an early-morning cut.

Clients who wail had better be wary. It is one thing to employ a competent horticultural contractor, it is quite another to expect a contractor to price his schedule of rates on anything but the written specification.

Traditionally we have got by in horticulture with the minimum of writing. Good or bad, that is the way it has been.

In years past, writing out complicated botanical names in exact detail on a plant label was often the extent of the written word for many horticulturists.

Fig. 4.1   Limited use for the written word

COMMERCIAL COMPLEXITIES

In the 1970s the scene began to change with controlled environments in commercial glasshouses. Detailed and accurate records had to be kept. The profit and loss of an expensive glasshouse crop depended on the recording and manipulation of a multitude of factors – heat, light levels, carbon dioxide and nutrients; the list became endless. With that level of compexity, it is not surprising that computers quickly followed in the 1980s.

In amenity horticulture in the past there has never been that same need to document everything, or even put it all in writing.

Contract documents invariably related to the supply of plants or the construction of a landscape design scheme. Thus there were relatively few documents of an industrial standard. Each document was written for a specific purpose.

This had one big advantage. These documents were relatively concise and to the point. It is well worth studying a few of these documents, as they provide an easy introduction to contract formalities. The addendum at the end of this chapter contains the standard form of tender for the supply and delivery of plants. Like many such documents, it has been prepared and published by a committee comprising a number of relevant institutes and organisations (it can be obtained from the Horticultural Trades Association).

This short and concise document is a refreshing change from the voluminous grounds maintenance tenders which are the norm for local authority contracts. The key essentials of a tender document (conditions, specifications, time allowed for tendering, etc.) are contained within this standard contract. It is all there in potted form; it is also a most useful document for ordering plants.

It will be important for any contractor to supply good plants as part of his contract. Not only must they be of good quality, but they must be seen to be of good quality. Seeing is believing, or is it? It is very easy for two people to disagree about the quality of plants, some form of benchmark is necessary. Thus forms like 'The Supply and Delivery of Plants' will provide an essentially impartial measurement.

It is surprising how few specifications exist for plant supply. There are the British Standard specifications, but few relate specifically to plants and their adequacy for planting in public places.

Many a Parks Department has built up its reputation on the ability to provide the highest-quality plants. Flower displays are used to dazzle the local population. All Parks Managers will say that the flower displays are also planted in such a manner as to discourage the unwanted attentions of a minority of the local population. Abuse by vandals are but one of the perils facing public planting displays. Plants are needed that are not just of excellent quality, but also able to withstand an adverse environment: traffic fumes, winter salt, dry summers, and the like.

THE PROVISION OF PLANTS

Perhaps the provision of adequate bedding plants is the ultimate test of a tender document, and also the ultimate test of confidence between two parties? Yet the quality of a plant can never be fully specified; before commitment, a client invariably will visit the supplying nursery and judge for himself.

Some Parks Managers may well try and hang onto their municipal nursery – it may prove easier to take away their status, than the nursey on which that status has been built. But like all else, the municipal nursery will go to tender. It has been decreed.

Alternative sources

This may lead eventually to the local garden centre becoming involved in tendering for grounds maintenance. Any contractor wishing to find a

Fig. 4.2   Razor-sharp on costs

secure local base need look no further, and an adequate supply of plants is assured. Or at least, so long as the specification is met in full.

The municipal nursery could become the seedbed of something different. Many nurseries must lend themselves to partnership ventures. Take the business acumen of a local garden centre, linked to the valued expertise of the parks nursery: that has to be a strong combination.

Any contractor, public or private, needs to accurately evaluate nursery provision. Very few municipal nurseries are competitive – on price, while commercial glasshouse horticulture is nothing if not razor-sharp on costs.

Years of sustained technical and managerial advancement have seen to that. Or you could say that years of fierce free market competition has led to those economies. Competitors from home and abroad have forced glasshouse horticulture in the UK to be intensively price competitive. Perhaps similar economies will follow from a free trade in grounds maintenance.

The municipal nursery, and civic pride

That may, or may not, be the case. However, it is quite clear that the municipal nursery could be a major asset, or a massive liability, to any contractor. In the past the quality of plant production has been

Fig. 4.3 The mayor will still need cosseting

everything. Cost of production was not only unknown, it did not even feature in the reckoning. Many municipal nurseries have grown to their present state of excellence on the need to cosset the Lord Mayor!

The Lord Mayor will still need cosseting, of course, in the future. However, the supply of the plants will be at least cost. Given the ability of the house plant industry to produce excellent plants all the year round, there is no doubt that they should be able to cope easily with a few more special functions per year, and also with the floral decorations required in the mayor's parlour.

If a contractor can obtain his plant supplies from a cheaper source than the local authority's nursery, will he? The answer is obvious (left to his own free choice).

Regrettably, many municipal nurseries will wither. The massive change to become cost-effective in such a short time will prove impossible for many. To succeed in such a cost-effective industry will need a change to year-round production. Sufficient turnover is essential to meet costs and make a profit. All contractors, acutely aware of costs, will be aware of that.

Nevertheless, contractors will need to be able to supply good-quality plants, as determined by the client. The local authority nursery, or the local garden centre, must be obvious site locations for that supply. Such a business combination would benefit the nursery and the contractor as well.

The nursery as a business

There are other options open to an enterprising municipal nursery. Options include a management buy-out, workers' cooperatives and management sell-off, or a combination of all three. No doubt, there will be many attempts to retain the nursery.

If a local authority can operate an equity share scheme of house purchase for its tenants, then something similar should be possible on the employment side of its activities.

A merchant bank would certainly provide a financial advance, provided the whole enterprise was profit-oriented. Indeed, that will be the basis for all contractors in future – the profitable supply of plants.

No contractor, public or private, will be able to afford to keep a nursery as a loss leader.

There is no point in providing the best plants at a loss. No single part of the grounds maintenance contract can be allowed to operate at a loss.

Hidden subsidy is perhaps the most corrosive factor in any business. A hidden subsidy occurs when part of the total business is running at a loss, without being seen. That part of the business is thus in receipt of a hidden subsidy.

What value is a nursery if it needs to be subsidized by the rest of the horticultural contract? Grounds maintenance contracts will not be that profitable, whoever operates them.

So the contractor will need to strike a balance between the source of plant supply compared to the cost. The quality of plants demanded will be the main criterion to satisfy. All authorities will demand the best.

And, again, that brings us back to the paperwork. The contractor will seek to supply only the quality of plants demanded in the written order or specification. If a salvia is requested, a salvia will be supplied.

If the contractor is to be successful, he will supply the smallest box-grown salvia he can find.

SPECIFICATION

It is for the client to specify the exact quality, shape, size, colour, variety, method of growing, etc. Then the contractor has to comply.

The clients specification will be in writing. It will undoubtedly refer to the Horticultural Trades Association (HTA) Form of Tender, and the relevant British Standard. Furthermore, there will be site visits to the nursery of supply. Samples may well be taken for future reference.

In this most sensitive of areas, client scrutiny will be paramount.

The supply of plants shows, in miniature, the whole of the tendering and contractor process. Tender, specifications, conditions, assessment of standards both before and after delivery – it is all there.

THE CONDITIONS OF CONTRACT

It is now worth concentrating on the conditions. The Conditions of Contract legally bind the contractor to supply exactly what, where and when the client dictates. Take an example for the supply of pot-grown salvias. The specification may demand that the highest-quality plants will be supplied. This is to be a plant grown in a 5" pot, and will have five fully formed flower spikes, at the time of delivery. The Conditions will ensure that the contractor supplies – or the penalties of the contract will be invoked.

After the appraisal of tenderers and the specification (both covered in previous chapters), the Conditions of Contract are the next most important part of any tender document. The Conditions of Contract govern the operation of that contract, for the length of the contract (of between three and six years).

For reference, an outline set of conditions is supplied in Appendix A4 at the end of this book.

CLIENT PREPARATION

Many tenders are in fact drawn up by a mix-and-match process. For example, the local authority in preparing a tender may have used the Conditions from the Association of Metropolitan Authorities; the Tenderer Appraisal from the Institute of Leisure and Amenity Management; and its own Specification. Provided all have been correctly combined, the contract will be binding on the contractor.

It is always time well spent for a contractor to check all written details. Many contractors make their profit from a multitude of justifiable claims.

THE DOCUMENTS IN PRACTICE

The Conditions, however, are only as good as the Specification or supporting documents. The Conditions and the Specification (although quite separate in the tender) will be totally intertwined in working practice.

The Conditions are a tool, like a garden fork or spade. The Specification is like the growing medium or compost. No matter how good the garden fork (or the gardener, for that matter), nothing much will grow in pure sand. So, if the Specification is lacking in body, the contractor need have little to worry about.

However, most Specifications will be extremely thorough. Full, detailed specifications will be the order of the day. Equally important, there will be constant reference to other supporting documents.

BRITISH STANDARDS

For example, the relevant British Standards will be quoted in most specifications. Having said that, it is sad to see so few British Standards of particular relevance to grounds maintenance. (Some of the most important British Standards are summarized in Appendix B at the end of this book). Most British Standards are limited to the supply of plants and landscape construction works. Maintenance in horticulture by contract has not until now been an important feature.

VARIATIONS AND NEGOTIATION

As regards specifications, then, British Standards are of limited assistance. This will increase the importance of the actual Specification itself. If the Specification is insufficiently detailed, then a flow of variation orders can be expected to follow. A good contractor will constantly seek variations if a different standard is requested from that which is detailed in the Specification.

However, the client will always retain the upper hand. He will be able to call in another contractor if he fails with the main contractor. There are limits to negotiations.

A contractor needs to be sensitive to the limits of his negotiating strength. That all comes back to the need for mutual confidence between contractor and client. Without confidence, and without agreement, a contract becomes impossible to manage. There is only one loser at the end of the day – namely, the contractor himself.

So bargain, claim, negotiate, even contest, but keep within the rules. Keep to the written word. That is the basis of the contract.

If the written word is wrong, inaccurate or insufficient to describe the exact work required, then a claim is justified.

A contractor's price is based on the words stated in the tender document. If those words prove to be inadequate for the task, then obviously the contractor will be faced with extra expense: a claim for extra expenses is totally justified.

SUMMARY

We have concentrated in this chapter on the need for accurate paperwork. Accurate specifications lead to highest standards and a close, easy working relationship between contractor and client. The principal points are:

- Agreement and confidence are the basis of any good contract.
- Contractor and client need to constantly and conscientiously work together to keep a good and effective relationship.
- That relationship depends on accurate written descriptions of work required to be undertaken.
- If changes are required to the written word, more costs may be incurred by the contractor, for which he should demand extra payment.
- That is because the contractor will have tendered on the least-cost combination of men and machines to undertake the work.
- In the past most written documents in horticulture originated in the supply of plants, or landscape construction.
- The supply of high-quality plants will be a key feature of maintenance contracts (success here is essential).
- The municipal nursery, garden centre or local plant centre could offer a valuable base for a partnership venture.
- Otherwise the municipal nursery may wither away.
- A loss-making nursery could quickly lead to a loss-making contract.
- Perhaps the most cost-effective way of supplying good-quality plants is to buy in from specialist suppliers.
- Again, an accurate written description is essential.
- Next to the written specifications (or detailed descriptions of works required) come the Conditions of Contract.
- The Conditions of Contract are able to enforce the tender.
- Hopefully, mutual confidence will be the order of the day.
- Even so, works will have to be undertaken exactly as stated.
- Although the number of suitable British Standards are limited, they will prove a reliable and impartial source of specific detail.
- Some of the more important British Standards are summarized in Appendix B1 at the end of this book.

Municipal horticulture will never be the same again. The spoken word has been replaced by the written word. This will have a lasting impact. The dark secrets of the Victorian potting shed have gone forever; and that, at least, must be better for everyone seeking higher, uniform standards across the range of maintenance.

Moreover, the relatively minor contract forms which have sufficed in the past have now been replaced by heavy tomes of text and maintenance schedules. Success for client and contractor will depend on their ability to achieve goals via these documents.

ADDENDUM: SOME BRIEF TENDER DOCUMENTS

Reproduced here are two tender documents. They provide a brief, easily read introduction to the complete tender. The main principles embodied in these documents will be found in more comprehensive forms. They are reproduced by courtesy of the Horticultural Trades Association and the Joint Council of Landscape Industries. Both bodies wish to encourage use of these standard specialist forms for tender and quotation purposes.

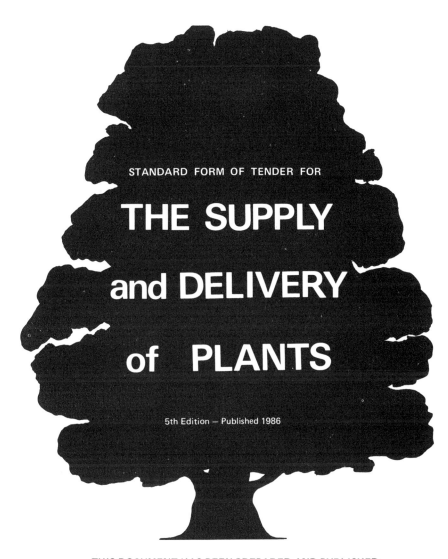

STANDARD FORM OF TENDER FOR

THE SUPPLY

and DELIVERY

of PLANTS

5th Edition — Published 1986

**THIS DOCUMENT HAS BEEN PREPARED AND PUBLISHED
BY THE COMMITTEE ON PLANT SUPPLY AND ESTABLISHMENT (CPSE)
AND APPROVED BY ITS CONSTITUENT BODIES:**

Arboricultural Association
Association of County Councils
Association of District Councils
Horticultural Trades Association

Institute of Chartered Foresters
Institute of Leisure & Amenity Management
Landscape Institute
National Farmers Union

IT IS RECOMMENDED TO BE USED FOR TENDERS FOR THE SUPPLY OF NURSERY STOCK

OBTAINABLE FROM:
THE HORTICULTURAL TRADES ASSOCIATION
19 HIGH STREET, THEALE, READING, BERKS. RG7 5AH Tel: (0734) 303132

GUIDANCE NOTES TO PURCHASER ON HOW TO PREPARE AND USE THIS FORM

1. PURPOSE

This form is intended for all types of enquiries for the supply and delivery of plants.

2. SPECIFICATION

When describing the type and size of plant required, ensure that:—

(a) Container grown plants are marked by the abbreviation "CG" (unless so marked it will be assumed that plants are either bare-rooted or balled).

(b) The designation where applicable and critical dimensions are stated.
The critical dimensions are:—

Younger trees	Height from ground level — see table below
Standard trees	Circumference of stem — see table below
Container grown nursery stock	Volume of container — see current British Container Growers Standards for container grown plants, garden or amenity grades as appropriate (available free from the Horticultural Trades Association at address on cover of this form).
Other upright growing shrubs and conifers	) Height from) ground) level
Other spreading shrubs & ground cover plants	))) Diameter)

(c) Clear stem heights of standard trees are stated if required to be in excess of 1.8m.

(d) Minimum stem diameters are stated if required for those plants so specified in BS 3936 Nursery Stock Part 4. Specification for Forest Trees.

3. QUANTITIES

Quantities of each variety should be totalled so the variety is entered once only in the Schedule of Quantities. It is recommended that large quantities be rounded off.

4. TYPING OF SCHEDULE OF QUANTITIES

Trees, shrubs, roses and herbaceous plants etc., should be listed separately, and in alphabetical order. Type the plant name and form or size high up in the appropriate box so as to allow any substitutes to be named clearly, should they be permitted. Where the schedule of quantities is prepared as a computer print-out, ensure it incorporates all the headings in the schedule of quantities in this form, and is similarly spaced.

5. PACKAGING

Any requirements additional to the specification in The Plant Handling Booklet published by the Committee on Plant Supply and Establishment July 1985 should be clearly stated. It must be recognised that these will be charged for as extras at cost.

6. TENDER FORM

Ensure all the asterisked items on the standard form of tender page are either completed or deleted.

7. NUMBER OF COPIES

It is essential that two copies be sent to each supplier requested to quote, so that one copy may be retained on file. Similarly computerised forms should be sent in duplicate. The reply envelope should be included with the enquiry and indicate to whom to be returned, closing date, and time for submission of tenders.

8. TIME ALLOWED FOR TENDERING

It is essential to allow Suppliers a minimum of two clear working weeks in which to tender, and a period of three weeks is recommended.

9. INSPECTION

Experience has shown that the best way of relating prices tendered by several Suppliers to the quality of the stock offered is by inspection — this is strongly recommended, and should be strictly by appointment.

10. ORDERING

It is strongly recommended that orders are placed as soon as possible after the closing date so as to ensure supply.

DIMENSIONS OF TREES

Additions to British Standards are indicated in **BOLD TYPE**

Relevant British Standard	Description		Circumference of stem measured 1.00m from ground level	Height from ground level	Clear stem height from ground level to lowest branch
BS3936 Part 4 Specification for Forest Trees	Seedling Seedling Undercut Seedling Undercut Seedling Transplant Transplant	Age (1+0) (2+0) (1u1) (1u2) (1+1) (1+2)	Does not apply	**15 — 30cm** **30 — 45cm** **45 — 60cm** **60 — 90cm** **90 — 120cm**	Does not apply
BS3936 Nursery stock Part 1. Specification for Trees & Shrubs	Whip (Shall have been previously transplanted at least once in its life, shall not necessarily be staked, and shall be without significant feather growth and without head).		Does not apply	1.20 — 1.50m 1.50 — 1.80m 1.80 — 2.10m 2.10 — 2.50m	Does not apply
BS3936 Nursery stock Part 1. Specification for Trees & shrubs	Feathered (Shall have been previously transplanted at least once in its life, shall have a defined reasonably straight upright central leader, and a stem furnished with evenly spread and balanced lateral shoots down to near ground level, according to its species).		Does not apply	**1.50 — 1.80m** 1.80 — 2.10m 2.10 — 2.50m 2.50 — 3.00m 3.00 — 3.50m	Does not apply

elevant British tandard	Description	Circumference of stem measured 1.00m from ground level	Height from ground level	Clear stem height from ground level to lowest branch
S3936 ursery stock art 1. pecification or Trees & hrubs	Short standard	not specified	not specified	1.00 — 1.20m
	Half standard	not specified	1.80 — 2.10m	1.20 — 1.50m
	Extra light standard	4 — 6 cm	2.10 — 2.50m	1.50 — 1.80m
	Light Standard	6 — 8 cm	2.50 — 2.75m	1.50 — 1.80m
	Standard	8 — 10 cm	2.75 — 3.00m	1.80m min.
	Tall Standard	8 — 10 cm	3.00 — 3.50m	1.80m min.
	Selected standard	10 — 12 cm	3.00 — 3.50m	1.80m min.
	Weeping trees — as above but height from ground level does not apply			
S5236 ecommendations r cultivation nd planting of ees in Advanced ursery Stock ategory	Heavy standard	12 — 14 cm	3.50 — 4.25m	1.80m min.
	Extra heavy standard	14 — 16 cm	4.25 — 6.00m	1.80m min.
	" " "	16 — 18 cm	4.50 — 6.25m	1.80m min.
	" " "	18 — 20 cm	4.50 — 6.50m	1.80m min.
S4043 ecommendations or Transplanting emi-Mature Trees	Semi Mature	20 — 75 cm	6.00 — 12.00m	to be specified

ENERAL CONDITIONS

GENERAL SPECIFICATION: The nursery stock must comply in all respects with the current relevant editions of British Standards except for trees in BS3936 Parts 1 and 4 and in BS5236 for which provisions extending those in British Standards are incorporated in this document. All container grown nursery stock is to comply with the current edition of British Container Growers Standards for Container grown plants. (Obtainable free from the Horticultural Trades Association at address on cover of this form).

COUNTRY WHERE GROWN: The country where grown is to be stated by the Supplier in the Schedule of Quantities. Plants grown in Britain for one growing season or longer shall be considered British grown.

INSPECTION: The purchaser reserves the right to inspect the stock by appointment.

FAIR WAGES: The supplier shall pay rates of wages and observe hours and conditions of labour not less favourable than those established for the trade or industry in the district where the work is carried out.

PARTIAL ORDERS: The purchaser reserves the right to accept offers in whole or in part. It is accepted that the Supplier will re-negotiate rates where (a) the quantity of a variety ordered differs significantly from the quantity quoted. (b) the value of the order placed differs significantly from the value of the original offer.

ORDER: No plants are to be supplied except on receipt of a duly signed official order. The purchaser is not bound to accept the lowest or any offer.

SUBSTITUTES: Where stocks are not available on receipt of order substitutes may only be made by mutual agreement.

PLANT HANDLING: Packaging and transporting shall be as specified in the booklet on Plant Handling published by the Committee on Plant Supply and Establishment July 1985. Plant handling from lifting until delivery on site shall be as recommended in this booklet.

DELIVERY:
(a)   Delivery is to be by the date specified by the purchaser, subject to exceptionally adverse weather or other factors beyond the supplier's control. The supplier is to advise in advance of the week of delivery and for sites not continuously manned to give 48 hours notice of the date and time of delivery. Delivery is to be during normal working hours. Delivery is to be to the one location specified except where otherwise stated, and may be signed for as unexamined.

(b)   In the event of the supplier failing to deliver the whole or part of an order by the date specified, for reasons other than exceptionally adverse weather or other factors beyond the supplier's control, the purchaser may give notice in writing that if delivery is not made within 10 working days from the date of receipt of such notice, or such other later date as the purchaser may specify, the purchaser will then cancel his order for the non-delivered items only, and pay others to supply them. All costs incurred thereby by him may be deducted from any monies due, or to become due to suppliers under this order, together with an additional 10% of the value of the non-delivered items as liquidated and ascertained damages in respect of direct loss and expense incurred by the purchaser, or shall be recoverable from the supplier by the purchaser as a debt.

COMPLAINTS: Complaints regarding quantity, quality or condition on delivery must be made in writing within 7 days of receipt of the goods. The purchaser has the right to return, at the supplier's expense, any plants supplied not to specification.

PAYMENT: Invoices are due for monthly settlement. Invoices may be rendered for each consignment. Prices quoted are strictly nett and are inclusive of delivery. Value Added Tax will be charged at the rates ruling at the time of delivery.

POSTPONED DELIVERIES: Postponement by the purchaser of the delivery of any plants after the agreed date until the following planting season shall be subject to a surcharge of 25% of the cost of each postponed item, or the supplier shall be reimbursed any direct loss and/or expense he has incurred as a consequence, which ever is the greater.

ARBITRATION: In the event of a dispute on an order based on these General Conditions, either party may contact one of the subscribing bodies, named on the front cover of this form, who will ask the President of the Institute of Arbitrators to appoint an Arbitrator.

SPECIAL CONDITIONS: Any special conditions or requirements are to be clearly stated. It must be recognised that these may incur an additional cost.

THE PURCHASER MUST COMPLETE OR DELETE ALL ASTERISKED ITEMS IN THIS FORM AS APPROPRIATE

STANDARD FORM OF TENDER FOR THE SUPPLY AND DELIVERY OF PLANTS

To be completed by the Purchaser

To (Name of Purchaser) _____   Ref. No. _____

Address _____   Contact Name _____

_____   Telephone _____

Project _____   Telex _____

Date _____

* Delivery to the site at _____   which will/will not* be continuously manned
if manned, name of person to contact on site

_____   _____

* The plants will be collected by prior arrangement.

Delivery date: Autumn 198........../Spring 198........... _____ (date and time as specified)*

THIS TENDER TO BE RETURNED NOT LATER THAN _____ (date and time).

To be completed by the Supplier
SUMMARY OF TENDER

Page No.	£	p	Page No.	£	p	Page No.	£	p
1			B/f:			B/f:		
2			6			10		
3			7					
4			8			Special cond. charge (if any)		
5			9			Delivery charge (if any)		
C/f:			C/f:			TOTAL:		

VAT additional:

✱ EITHER

Subject to an order being received within 5 working days of the date for submission of this tender, for all the items quoted on our tender, and subject to our not advising the purchaser to the contrary within 3 working days of receipt of such order, we undertake to supply/supply and deliver* the plants shown on the attached pages numbered 1 to .... in accordance with the General Conditions for the sum of £........................pounds .... pence (amount in words) exclusive of any Value Added Tax due in accordance with the Finance (No. 2) Act 1975, or subsequent re-enactment.

In the event of an order not being received within 5 working days, this tender remains open for acceptance within a further 4 weeks, subject to the plants being unsold on receipt of order.
If the plants are to be supplied through a contractor whose identity is not known to us at the time of tender, we reserve the right to withdraw this tender within 14 days of the name of the contractor being made known to us.

✱ OR

Subject to the plants being unsold on receipt of order, we undertake to supply/supply and deliver* the plants shown on the attached pages numbered 1 to .... in accordance with the General Conditions for the sum of £................................. pounds .... pence (amount in words) exclusive of any Value Added Tax due in accordance with the Finance (No. 2) Act 1975 or subsequent re-enactment.

This tender is open for acceptance within 5 weeks from the date for submission of this tender.
If the plants are to be supplied through a contractor whose identity is not known to us at the time of tender, we reserve the right to withdraw this tender within 14 days of the name of the contractor being made known to us.

Date _____   Signed _____
(For and on behalf of the Supplier)

Tel: _____   Contact Name _____

Telex: _____   Name of Supplier _____

Ref. No. _____

Address: _____

SCHEDULE OF QUANTITIES

Type plant names in the upper space to allow any alternative to be inserted by the supplier in the lower space, should substitutes be permitted.

To: (Name of Purchaser)...

Item No.	Plant Name	Country where grown (to be stated by supplier)	Designation & critical dimension (size or volume)	Quantity	Rate £	TOTAL £
1						
2						
3						
4						
5						
6						
7						
8						
9						
10						
11						
12						
13						
14						
15						

Name of Supplier:

....

Page total carried forward to summary sheet............. £

SCHEDULE OF QUANTITIES

Type plant names in the upper space to allow any alternative to be inserted by the supplier in the lower space, should substitutes be permitted.

To: (Name of Purchaser)...

Item No.	Plant Name	Country where grown (to be stated by supplier)	Designation & critical dimension (size or volume)	Quantity	Rate £	TOTAL £
16						
17						
18						
19						
20						
21						
22						
23						
24						
25						
26						
27						
28						
29						
30						

Name of Supplier:

....

Page total carried forward
to summary sheet.............   £

Joint Council of Landscape Industries Contract

Now it is hereby agreed as follows

Article 1
For the consideration hereinafter mentioned the Contractor will in accordance with the Contract Documents carry out and complete the Works.

Article 2
The Employer will pay to the Contractor the sum of _____

_____

_____ (£ _____)

exclusive of VAT or such other sum as shall become payable hereunder at the times and in the manner specified in the Contract Documents.

Article 3
The term "Landscape Architect" in the said Conditions shall mean

_____

or in the event of his death or ceasing to be the Landscape Architect for the purpose of this Contract such other person as the Employer shall within 14 days of the death or cessation as aforesaid nominate for that purpose, provided that no person subsequently appointed to be the Landscape Architect under this Contract shall be entitled to disregard or overrule any certificate or instruction given by the Landscape Architect for the time being.

Article 4
If any dispute or difference as to the construction of this Agreement or any matter or thing of whatsoever nature arising thereunder or in connection therewith, except under the Supplementary Memorandum Part B clause B6 *(Value Added Tax)* or Part C *(Statutory tax deduction scheme)* to the extent provided in clause C8, shall arise between the Employer or the Landscape Architect on his behalf and the Contractor either during the progress or after the abandonment of the Works or after the determination of the employment of the Contractor it shall be and is hereby referred to arbitration in accordance with clause 9. If under clause 9·1 the Employer and the Contractor have not agreed a person as the Arbitrator the appointor of the Arbitrator shall be the President or a Vice-President for the time being of the Landscape Institute.

As witness the hands of the parties hereto

Signed for and on behalf of the Employer _____

(For the Employer)

in the presence of _____

(Witness)

Signed for and on behalf of the Contractor _____

(For the Contractor)

in the presence of _____

(Witness)

Contents

Note:
*Clauses marked * should be completed/deleted*
as appropriate
†see note on page 8

·0 Intentions of the parties

Contractor's obligation

·1 The Contractor shall with due diligence and in a good and workmanlike manner carry out and complete the Works in accordance with the Contract Documents using materials and workmanship of the quality and standards therein specified provided that where and to the extent that approval of the quality of materials or of the standards of workmanship is a matter for the opinion of the Landscape Architect such quality and standards shall be to the reasonable satisfaction of the Landscape Architect.

Landscape Architect's duties

·2 The Landscape Architect shall issue any further information necessary for the proper carrying out of the Works, issue all certificates and confirm all instructions in writing in accordance with these Conditions.

Contract Bills and SMM

·3 Where the Contract Documents include Contract Bills, the Contract Bills unless otherwise expressly stated therein in respect of any specified item or items are to have been prepared in accordance with the Standard Method of Measurement of Building Works, 7th Edition, published by the Royal Institution of Chartered Surveyors and the Building Employers Confederation (formerly National Federation of Building Trades Employers).

2·0 Commencement and completion

Commencement and completion

·1 The Works may be commenced on

....
and shall be completed by

....

Extension of contract period

2·2 If it becomes apparent that the Works will not be completed by the date for completion inserted in clause 2·1 hereof (or any later date fixed in accordance with the provisions of this clause 2·2) for reasons beyond the control of the Contractor including compliance with any instruction of the Landscape Architect under this contract whose issue is not due to a default of the Contractor, then the Contractor shall so notify the Landscape Architect who shall make, in writing, such extension of the time for completion as may be reasonable.

Damages for non-completion

2·3 If the Works are not completed by the completion date inserted in clause 2·1 hereof or by any later completion date fixed under clause 2·2 hereof then the Contractor shall pay or allow to the Employer liquidated damages at the rate of £ .... per week for every week or part of a week between the aforesaid completion date of practical completion. The Employer may deduct such liquidated damages from any monies due to the Contractor under this contract or he may recover them from the Contractor as a debt.

Completion date

2·4 The Landscape Architect shall certify the date when in his opinion the Works have reached practical completion.

Defects liability

2·5 Any defects, excessive shrinkages or other faults, other than tree, shrub, grass and other plant failures, which appear within three months [b] .... of the date of practical completion and are due to materials or workmanship not in accordance with the Contract or frost occurring before practical completion shall be made good by the Contractor entirely at his own cost unless the Landscape Achitect shall otherwise instruct.

The Landscape Architect shall certify the date when in his opinion the Contractor's obligations under this clause 2·5 have been discharged.

Partial Possession by Employer

†2·6 If before practical completion of the Works the Employer with the consent of the Contractor shall take possession of any part then:

The date for possession of the part shall be the date of practical completion of the part and clause 4·3 shall apply to the part.

In lieu of the sum to be paid by the Contractor under clause 2·3 for any period during which the Works remain uncompleted after the Employers possession of any part the sum paid shall bear the same ratio to the sum stated in clause 2·3 as does the Contract Sum less the value of the part to the Contract Sum.

Failures of Plants (Pre-Practical Completion)

†2·7 Any trees, shrubs, grass or other plants, other than those found to be missing or defective as a result of theft or malicious damage and which shall be replaced as set out in clause 6·5 of these conditions, which are found to be or have been defective at practical completion of the works shall be replaced by the Contractor entirely at his own cost unless the Landscape Architect shall otherwise instruct. The Landscape Architect shall certify the dates when in his opinion the Contractor's obligations under this clause have been discharged.

(Post-Practical Completion)

*A The maintenance of trees, shrubs, grass and other plants after the date of the said certificate will be carried out by the Contractor for the duration of the periods stated in accordance with the programme and in the manner specified in the Contract Documents. Any grass which is found to be defective within .... months, any shrubs, ordinary nursery stock trees ot other plants found to be defective within .... months and any trees, semi-mature advanced or extra large nursery stock found to be defective within .... months of the date of Practical Completion and are due to materials or workmanship not in accordance with the contract shall be replaced by the Contractor entirely at his own cost unless the Landscape Architect shall otherwise instruct. The Landscape Architect shall certify the dates when in his opinion the Contractor's obligations under this clause have been discharged.

*B The maintenance of the trees, shrubs, grass and other plants after the date of the said certificate will be undertaken by the Employer who will be responsible for the replacement of any trees, shrubs, grass or other plants which are subsequently defective.

---

[b]   If a different period is required delete 'three months' and insert the appropriate period.

*   Delete (A) or (B) as appropriate.

3·0 Control of the Works

Assignment

3·1 Neither the Employer nor the Contractor shall, without the written consent of the other, assign this Contract.

Sub-contracting

3·2 The Contractor shall not sub-contract the Works or any part thereof without the written consent of the Landscape Architect whose consent shall not unreasonably be withheld.

Contractor's representative

3·3 The Contractor shall at all reasonable times keep upon the Works a competent person in charge and any instructions given to him by the Landscape Architect shall be deemed to have been issued to the Contractor.

Exclusion from the Works

3·4 The Landscape Architect may (but not unreasonably or vexatiously) issue instructions requiring the exclusion from the Works of any person employed thereon.

Landscape Architect's instructions

3·5 The Landscape Architect may issue written instructions which the Contractor shall forthwith carry out. If instructions are given orally they shall, in two days, be confirmed in writing by the Landscape Architect.

If within 7 days after receipt of a written notice from the Landscape Architect requiring compliance with an instruction the Contractor does not comply therewith then the Employer may employ and pay other persons to carry out the work and all costs incurred thereby may be deducted by him from any monies due or to become due to the Contractor under this Contract or shall be recoverable from the Contractor by the Employer as a debt.

Variations

†3·6 The Landscape Architect may, without invalidating the contract, order an addition to or omission from or other change in the Works or the order or period in which they are to be carried out and any such instruction shall be valued by the Landscape Architect on a fair and reasonable basis, using where relevant, prices in the priced specification/schedules/Bills of Quantity/schedule of rates [c] and such valuation shall include any direct loss and/or expense incurred by the Contractor due to the regular progress of the Works being affected by compliance with such instruction.

If any omission substantially varies the scope of the work such valuation shall take due account of the effect on any remaining items of work.

† Instead of the valuation referred to above, the price may be agreed between the Landscape Architect and the Contractor prior to the Contractor carrying out any such instruction.

P.C. and Provisional sums

3·7 The Landscape Architect shall issue instructions as to the expenditure of any P.C. and provisional sums and such instructions shall be valued by the price agreed in accordance with clause 3·6 hereof.

Objections to a Nomination

†3·8 The Landscape Architect shall not nominate any person as a nominated sub-contractor against whom the Contractor shall make reasonable objection or who will not enter into a sub-contract that applies the appropriate provisions of these conditions.

4.0 Payment

Correction of inconsistencies

4·1 Any inconsistency in or between the Contract Drawings [c] and the Contract Specification [c] and the schedules [c] shall be corrected and any such correction which results in an addition omission or other change shall be treated as a variation under clause 3·6 hereof. Nothing contained in the Contract Drawings [c] or the Contract Specification [c] or the schedules or the Bills of Quantity [c] or the Schedule of Rates [c] shall override, modify or affect in any way what soever the application or interpretation of that which is contained in these Conditions.

Progress payments and retention

4.2* The Landscape Architect shall if requested by the Contractor, at intervals of not less than four weeks calculated from the date for commence ment subject to any agreement between the parties as to stage payments, certify progress payments to the Contractor, in respect of the value of the Works properly executed, including any amounts either ascertained or agreed under clauses 3·6 and 3·7 hereof, and the value of any materials and goods which have been reason ably and properly brought upon the site for the purpose of the Works and which are adequately stored and protected against the weather and other casualties less a retention of 5% (. . . . . %) [e] and less any sums previously certified, and the Employer shall pay to the Contractor the amount so certified within 1 days of the date of the certificate.

Penultimate certificate

†4·3 The Landscape Architect shall within 14 days after the date of practical completion certified under clause 2·4 hereof certify payment to the Contractor of 97½% of the total amount to be paid to the Contractor under this contract so far as that amount is ascertainable at the date of practical completion, including any amount either ascertained or agreed under clauses 3·6 and 3·7 hereof less the amount of any progress payments previously certified to the Employer and less the cost of any subsequent mainten ance included in the contract in accordance with Clause 2·7A unless the failures of plants as set out in clause 2·7 are in excess of 10% in which case the amount retained shall be adjusted accordingly, and the Employer shall pay to the Contractor the amount so certified within 1 days of that certificate.

Final certificate

4·4 The Contractor shall supply within three months/ . . . . [d] from the date of practical completion all documentation reasonably required for the computation of the amount to be finally certified by the Landscape Architect and the Landscape Architect shall within 28 days of receipt of such documentation provided that the Landscape Architect has issued the certificate under clause 2·5 and 2·7 hereof, issue a final certificate certifying the amount remaining due to the Contractor or due to the Employer as the case may be and such sum shall as from the fourteenth day after the date of the final certificate be a debt payable as the case may be by the Employer to the Contrac tor or by the Contractor to the Employer.

---

[c] Delete as appropriate to follow any deletions in the recital on page 1.

[d] If a different period is required delete 'three months' and insert the appropriate percentage period.

[e] If a different percentage is required delete 5% and insert the appropriate retention %.

Contribution, levy and tax changes [f]

5 Contribution, levy and tax changes shall be dealt with by the application of Part A of the Supplementary Memorandum to the Agreement for Landscape Works. The percentage addition under part A, clause A5 is . . . . % [e].

Fixed price [f]

5A No account shall be taken in any payment to the Contractor under this Contract of any change in the cost to the Contractor of the labour, materials, plant and other resources employed in carrying out the Works except as provided in clause 4·5 hereof, if applicable.

Fluctuations [f]

5B The Contract sum shall be adjusted in accordance with the provisions of Part D of the Supplementary Memorandum and the Formula Rules current at the date stated in the tender documents, and which shall be incorporated in all certificates except those relating to the release of retention and shall be exclusive of any Value Added Tax. These provisions shall also be incorporated as appropriate in any sub contract agreement.

0 Statutory obligations

Statutory obligations, notices, fees and charges

1 The Contractor shall comply with, and give all notices required by, any statute, any statutory instrument, rule or order or any regulation or byelaw applicable to the Works (hereinafter called 'the statutory requirements') and shall pay all fees and charges in respect of the Works legally recoverable from him. If the Contractor finds any divergence between the statutory requirements and the contract documents or between the statutory requirements and any instruction of the Landscape Architect he shall immediately give to the Landscape Architect, a written notice specifying the divergence. Subject to this latter obligation, the Contractor shall not be liable to the Employer under this Contract if the Works do not comply with the statutory requirements where and to the extent that such non-compliance of the Work results from the Contractor having carried out work in accordance with the Contract Documents or any instruction of the Landscape Architect.

Value Added Tax

2 The sum or sums due to the Contractor under Article 2 hereof this Agreement shall be exclusive of any Value Added Tax and the Employer shall pay to the Contractor any Value Added Tax properly chargeable by the Commissioners of Custom and Excise on the supply to the Employer of any goods and services by the Contractor under this Contract in the manner set out in Part B of the Supplementary Memorandum to the Agreement for Landscape Works.

Statutory tax deduction scheme

3 Where at the date of tender the Employer was a 'contractor', or where at any time up to the issue and payment of the final certificate the Employer becomes a 'contractor', for the purposes of the statutory tax deduction scheme referred to in Part C of the Supplementary Memorandum to the Agreement for Landscape Works, Part C of that Memorandum shall be operated.

4 Number not used

Prevention of corruption

5·5 If the Employer is a local authority he shall be entitled to cancel this contract and to recover from the Contractor the amount of any loss resulting from such cancellation, if the Contractor shall have offered or given or agreed to give to any person any gift or consideration of any kind or if the Contractor shall have committed any offence under the Prevention of Corruption Acts 1889 to 1916 or shall have given any fee or reward the receipt of which is an offence under sub-section (2) of section 117 of the Local Government Act 1972 or any re-enactment thereof.

6·0 Injury, damage and insurance

Injury to or death of persons

6·1 The Contractor shall be liable for and shall indemnify the Employer against any expense, liability, loss, claim or proceedings whatsoever arising under any statute or at common law in respect of personal injury to or death of any person whomsoever arising out of or in the course of or caused by the carrying out of the Works, except to the extent that the same is due to any act or neglect of the Employer or of any person for whom the Employer is responsible. Without prejudice to his liability to indemnify the Employer the Contractor shall take out and maintain and shall cause any sub-contractor to take out and maintain insurance which, in respect of liability to employees or apprentices shall comply with the Employer's Liability (Compulsory Insurance) Act 1969 and any statutory orders made thereunder or any amendment or re-enactment thereof and in respect of any other liability for personal injury or death shall be such as is necessary to cover the liability of the Contractor, or, as the case may be, of such sub-contractor.

Injury or damage to property

6·2 The Contractor shall be liable for, and shall indemnify the Employer against, any expense, liability, loss, claim or proceedings in respect of any injury or damage whatsoever to any property real or personal (other than injury or damage to the Works) insofar as such injury or damage arises out of or in the course of or by reason of the carrying out of the Works and to the extent that the same is due to any negligence, breach of statutory duty, omission or default of the Contractor, his servants or agents, or of any person employed or engaged by the Contractor upon or in connection with the Works or any part thereof, his servants or agents. Without prejudice to his obligation to indemnify the Employer the Contractor shall take out and maintain and shall cause any sub-contractor to take out and maintain insurance in respect of the liability referred to above in respect of injury or damage to any property real or personal other than the Works which shall be for an amount not less than the sum stated below for any one occurrence or series of occurrences arising out of one event:

insurance cover referred to above to be not less than: £ _____

---

[f] Delete clause 4·5 if the contract period is of such limited duration as to make the provisions of part A of the Supplementary Memorandum to this agreement inapplicable.

[g] Delete 6·3A or 6·3B as appropriate.
Where the Contractor has in force an All Risks Policy which insures the Works against loss or damage by, inter alia, the perils referred to in clause 6·3A this Policy may be used to provide the insurance required by clause 6·3A provided the Policy recognises the Employer as a joint insured with the Contractor in respect of the Works and the Policy is maintained.

[h] Percentage to be inserted.

Insurance of the Works — Fire etc. — New Works [g]

6·3A The Contractor shall in the joint names of Employer and Contractor insure against loss and damage by fire, lightning, explosion, storm, tempest, flood, bursting or overflowing of water tanks, apparatus or pipes, earthquake, aircraft and other aerial devices or articles dropped therefrom, riot and civil commotion, for the full reinstatement value of the Works thereof plus .... % [h] to cover professional fees, all work executed and all unfixed materials and goods intended for, delivered to, placed on or adjacent to the Works and intended therefore. After any inspection required by the insurers in respect of a claim under the insurance mentioned in this clause 6·3A the Contractor shall with due diligence restore or replace work or materials or goods damaged and dispose of any debris and proceed with and complete the Works. The Contractor shall not be entitled to any in respect of work or materials or goods damaged or the disposal of any debris other than the monies received under the said insurance (less the percentage to cover professional fees) and such monies shall be paid to the Contractor under certificates of the Landscape Architect at the periods stated in clause 4·0 hereof.

Insurance of the Works — Fire, etc. — Existing structure [g]

6·3B The Employer shall in the joint names of Employer and Contractor insure against loss or damage to the existing strucutres (together with the contents owned by him or for which he is responsible) and to the Works and all unfixed materials and goods intended for, delivered to, placed on or adjacent to the Works and intended therefore by fire, lightning, explosion, storm, tempest, flood, bursting or overflowing of water tanks, apparatus or pipes, earthquake, aircraft and other aerial devices or articles dropped therefrom, riot and civil commotion.

If any loss or damage as referred to in this clause occurs then the Landscape Architect shall issue instructions for the reinstatement and making good of such loss or damage in accordance with clause 3·5 hereof and such instructions shall be valued under clause 3·6 hereof.

Evidence of insurance

6·4 The Contractor shall produce, and shall cause any sub-contractor to produce, such evidence as the Employer may reasonably require that the insurances referred to in clauses 6·1 and 6·2 and, where applicable 6·3A, hereof have been taken out and are in force at all material times. Where clause 6·3B hereof is applicable the Employer shall produce such evidence as the Contractor may reasonably require that the insurance referred to therein has been taken out and is in force at all material times.

Malicious Damage or Theft (before Practical Completion)

†6·5A All loss or damage arising from any theft or malicious damage prior to practical completion shall be made good by the Contractor at his own expense.

B The Contract sum shall include the provisional sum of £ ....* to be expended as instructed by the Landscape Architect in respect of the cost of all work arising from any theft or malicious damage to the works beyond the control of the Contractor prior to practical completion of the works.

7·0 Determination

Determination by Employer

7·1 The Employer may, but not unreasonably vexatiously, by notice by registered post recorded delivery to the Contractor forthw determine the employment of the Contrac under this Contract if the Contractor shall ma default in any one or more of the followi respects:

1 if the Contractor without reasonable cau fails to proceed diligently with the Works wholly suspends the carrying out of Works before completion;

2 if the Contractor becomes bankrupt or mak any composition or arrangement with creditors, has a proposal in respect of company for a voluntary arrangement fo composition of debts or scheme of arrang ment approved in accordance with Insolvency Act 1986 in respect of company to the court for the appointment an administrator or has a winding up ord made or (except for the purposes of reco struction) a resolution for voluntary windi up passed or a receiver or manager of business or undertaking is duly appointed has an administrative receiver as defined the Insolvency Act 1986 appointed possession is taken by or on behalf of a creditor of any property the subject o charge.

In the event of the Employer determining employment of the Contractor as aforesaid Contractor shall immediately give up possessi of the site of the Works and the Employer sh not be bound to make any further payment the Contractor until after completion of Works. Provided always that the right determ ation shall be without prejudice to any oth rights or remedies which the Employer m possess.

Determination by Contractor

7·2 The Contractor may but not unreasonably vexatiously, by notice by registered post recorded delivery to the Employer forthw determine the employment of the Contrac under this Contract if the Employer shall ma default in any one or more of the followi respects:

1 if the Employer fails to make any progre payment due under the provisions clause 4·2 hereof within 14 days of su payment being due;

2 if the Employer or any person for whom he responsible interferes with or obstructs t carrying out of the Works or fails to make t site of the Works available for the Contract in accordance with clause 2·1 hereof;

3 if the Employer suspends the carrying out the Works for a continuous period of at le one month;

4 if the Employer becomes bankrupt or mak any composition or arrangement with creditors or has a proposal in respect of company for a voluntary arrangement fo composition of debts or scheme of arrang ment approved in accordance with t Insolvency Act 1986, or has an applicati made under the Insolvency Act 1986 respect of his company to the court for t

The amount to be inserted should take account of the Wo and the place where they are carried out. Delete [A] or [B appropriate.

appointment of an administrator, or has a winding up order made or (except for the purposes of reconstruction) a resolution for voluntary winding-up passed or a receiver or manager of his business is duly appointed, or has an administrative receiver, as defined in the Insolvency Act 1986, appointed or possession is taken by or on behalf of any creditor of any property the subject of a charge.

Provided that the employment of the Contractor shall not be determined under clauses 7·2·1, 7·2·2 or 7·2·3 hereof unless the Employer has continued the default for seven days after receipt by registered post or recorded delivery of a notice from the Contractor specifying such default.

In the event of the Contractor determining the Employment of the Contractor as aforesaid the Employer shall pay to the Contractor, after taking into account amounts previously paid, such sum as shall be fair and reasonable for the value of work begun and executed, materials on site and the removal of all temporary buildings, plant, tools and equipment. Provided always that the right of determination shall be without prejudice to any other rights or remedies which the Contractor may possess.

Supplementary Memorandum

Meaning of references in 4·5, 4·6, 5·2 and 5·3
The references in clauses 4·5, 4·6, 5·2 and 5·3 to the Supplementary Memorandum to the Agreement for Landscape Works are to that issued for use with this Form by the Joint Council for Landscape Industries as endorsed hereon.

Settlement of disputes — Arbitration

When the Employer or the Contractor require a dispute of difference as referred to in Article 4 to be referred to arbitration then either the Employer or the Contractor shall give written notice to the other to such effect and such dispute or difference shall be referred to the arbitration and final decision of a person to be agreed between the parties as the Arbitrator, or, upon failure so to agree within 14 days after the date of the aforesaid written notice, of a person to be appointed as the Arbitrator on the request of either the Employer or the Contractor by the person named in Article 4.

Subject to the provisions of clause A4·3 in the Supplementary Memorandum, the Arbitrator shall, without prejudice to the generality of his powers, have power to rectify the Agreement so that it accurately reflects the true agreement made by the Employer and the Contractor, to direct such measurements and/or valuations as may in his opinion be desirable in order to determine the rights of the parties and to ascertain and award any sum which ought to have been the subject of or included in any certificate and to open up, review and revise any certificate,opinion, decision, requirement of notice and to determine all matters in dispute which shall be submitted to him in the same manner as if no such certificate, opinion, decision, requirement or notice had been given.

The award of such Arbitrator shall be final and binding on the parties.

9·4 If before making his final award the Arbitrator dies or otherwise ceases to act as the Arbitrator, the Employer and the Contractor shall forthwith appoint a further Arbitrator, or, upon failure so to appoint within 14 days of any such death of cessation, then either the Employer or the Contractor may request the person named in Article 4 to appoint such further Arbitrator. Provided that no such further Arbitrator shall be entitled to disregard any direction of the previous Arbitrator or to vary or revise any award of the previous Arbitrator except to the extent that the previous Arbitrator had power so to do under the JCT Arbitration Rules and/or with the agreement of the parties and/or by the operation of law.

9·5 [1·2] The arbitration shall be conducted in accordance with the 'JCT Arbitration Rules' current at the date of this Agreement [1·2]. Provided that if any amendments to the Rules so current have been issued by the Joint Contracts Tribunal after the aforesaid date the Employer and the Contractor may, by a joint notice in writing to the Arbitrator, state that they wish the arbitration to be conducted in accordance with the JCT Arbitration Rules as so amended.

[1·1]   The JCT Arbitration Rules contain stricter time limits that those prescribed by some arbitration rules or those frequently observed in practice. The parties should note that a failure by a party or the agent of a party to comply with the time limits incorporated in these Rules may have adverse consequences.

[1·2]   Delete clause 9·5 if it is not to apply.

January 1989 revision

Dated _____ 19 ____

Agreement for Landscape Works

(In Scotland when English Law is not to apply supplementary clauses in respect of Building Regulations and Arbitration may be required)

First issued April 1978, revised April 1981
reprinted with corrections April 1982
revised April 1985, reprinted with corrections
September 1986. Clause related to insurance
provisions, revised September 1987.
Revised January 1989.

Between _____

_____

and _____

_____

This Form is issued by the
Joint Council for Landscape Industries
comprising:-

Landscape Institute
Horticultural Trades Association
British Association Landscape Industries
National Farmers' Union
Institute of Leisure and Amenity Management.

†Note: All clauses other than those marked † are similar to those in the Joint Contracts Tribunal Agreement for Minor Building Works.

Published for the Joint Council for Landscape
Industries by the Landscape Institute
12 Carlton House Terrace, London SW1Y 5AH and
available from RIBA Publications Limited
66 Portland Place, London W1N 4AD.
© JCLI April 1985

Printed by Duolith Ltd.
Welwyn Garden City, Herts.

First issued April 1978

The Joint Council for Landscape Industries has issued a Supplementary Memorandum for use with this Form, where applicable, as referred to in the list of Contents on page 3 and in clause 8·1. The Supplementary Memorandum is attached.

The Council previously issued Practice Note No. 1 & Practice Note No. 2, but both are superseded by Practice Note No. 3 which is attached.

The complete document now comprises 3 items:
Form of Agreement for Landscape Works.
Supplementary Memorandum.
JCLI Practice Note No. 3.
The Supplementary Memorandum and
Practice Note No. 3 may be torn off as convenient.

Chapter Five

Time and costs

The kernel of a tender submission for any contract is accurate pricing. Given the opportunity to tender, a contractor obviously wins or loses by the price submitted.

HOURLY RATES

A contractor's price needs to include all his costs; therefore, he will need to allocate all his costs on to his wage bill. In this manner, he can be sure of covering all his fixed and variable costs.
An hourly rate is therefore built up from:

- wage payments to the workforce;
- National Insurance, sick pay and holiday pay, other employee on-costs, etc.;
- office and administration on-costs;
- vehicle and machinery costs;
- overheads such as the depot-running costs;
- an element for profit.

Every landscape contractor will know exactly his hourly rates. That hourly rate will be used to determine the costs of each job within a tender document.

However, it is also advisable to check if the workrate per hour is adequate. Many a slip is made here.

It is all too easy in office estimating to get wrapped up in the fine detail yet forget the fundamental realities of the exercise. Accurate estimating complements high output.

THE MYTH OF THE 40-HOUR WORKING WEEK

If productivity is low, no amount of estimating will win a tender. Most landscape contractors work a 40-hour week, approximately. Fine, but that is the theory. No doubt everyone believes he works a 40-hour week (often much more) – but is it true? Of course, it is not. A person may be at work for 40 hours or more, but he cannot work for every minute of every hour. How long, then, does a person actually work?

Opinions vary. Anyone can be quite firm in his views about the theoretical 40-hour week. Being accurate about the actual number of working hours is something quite different: some will say 30 hours, others 35.

How many actually know? Very few; the man himself knows (if he bothered to count it one week), and the supervisor should also know. However, often the supervisor does not know, because in grounds maintenance, individual working is a strong feature. It has to be. There is little point in two men trying to mow a bowling-green. And even less for two men to work together just to keep an eye on each other. Horticulture and landscape maintenance have always provided a career for people with an individual streak – long may it remain. But if the individual gardener does not know how many hours he actually works, then what chance has the manager?

The 39-hour or 40-hour week becomes rather like the market trader's

Table 5.1   The lost time of A. Jones

		Hours
1	About 20 min on average to the actual site of work from the depot	
2	Four times a day, 5 days a week	6.25
	. . . that's nearly a day a week lost for starters	
3	Tea, personal needs	3.25
4	Annual leave, public holidays, sickness (averaged for all workers over the whole year)	9.50
	. . . there goes another day and more	
5	Day release	8.00
	. . . and another	
6	Leaning on the shovel	5.00
	. . . admit it, it's impossible to work all the time	
7	Collect wages	1.00
8	Fill in time sheets, vehicle sheets, job order tickets, cost control forms, etc.	1.00
		34.00

WORK, ONE HOUR A DAY LEFT!
Better come in on a Saturday morning, to actually get some work done.
On overtime, of course.

£5 knock-down offer. Yes, a real bargain, not £5...not £4...no, not even £2. It's all yours, including the wrapping, for just a £1 coin. With a clap of the hands, the bargain is struck and the cash is exchanged for goods. Everyone is happy. Unfortunately, with the 40-hour week, that is no good at all.

The 40-hour working week needs exposing for the myth that it certainly is. It may or may not be 40 hours, but working it certainly is not (Table 5.1). First at least 20 minutes needs to be allowed for the staff to travel to the worksite and back again for lunch, of course. That is almost one day a week lost, for a start. Now, allow half that time again for tea-breaks, and personal needs. One and a half days are now lost without even an inch of grass being cut.

Similarly, putting together all annual leave entitlements can be eye-opening. After adding on some allowance for sickness and public holidays, it will be seen that this all amounts to 20%. Yet another day of the week has slipped through a contractor's fingers!

Now add into the equation time off for day-release studies or trade union business. Then time must be allowed too for leaning on the proverbial shovel. This honours the traditional philosophy, never let the gaffer catch you without a shovel in your hand! Also add on time to find the shovel in the first place (you may as well), and do not forget time for cleaning it.

The five-day week has gone.

TIME AND MONEY

Before the submission of any tender, accurate assessment of time and hourly costs need to be made. These assessments have to be based on facts. Otherwise the prices submitted will not be achieved.

It is one thing to win a tender, quite another to see the subsequent contract successfully through to the end of its three- to six-years' duration.

The importance of everyone involved in a contract being fully aware of how his time is spent cannot be overemphasized.

Therein lies success or failure. There is a rich reward for the person who can set a musical jingle to the theme, time is money. How quickly, though, it can slip between your fingers.

Each job and task within the tender will need to be individually priced. It is no good merely costing the actual time taken to undertake the job. Due allowance has to be built in for lost time. A highly accurate assessment of the actual productive hours is therefore essential for everyone.

ASSESSING LOST TIME

For successful estimating, it is necessary first to determine the actual hours per man spent on productive work.

If, due to travelling, etc., a man only spends 20 hours per week on productive work, then quite simply the hourly rate to be used in costing needs to be doubled. Each and every job will cost twice as much, compared to the man who spends 40 hours on productive work per week.

Wage war on lost time is the motto of the future.

Success depends on making accurate assessments of the actual lost time incurred by each man and team. That way, it can be truly reflected in the price.

So armed with the two major ingredients (hourly rates and job timings), a contractor is ready to start to price a tender.

There will be a whole diversity of horticultural maintenance required by each specific contract. This could range from greenkeeping and groundsmanship to the less-than-horticultural tasks of pavilion cleaning and many other tasks.

This is where an astute contractor's own acumen and judgement come to the forefront.

Knowledge of the best machinery and methods are needed. Tenders are, if nothing else, a competitive test of knowledge. The person who wins believes that he can deliver the service at least cost.

He believes he can find the best combination of men and machines to carry out the specification to the required standard at a price less than his competitors.

That is the basis of all free competition.

In the first part of the 1990s competition will be varied. Most tenders may, or may not, rest on fine judgements of technical skill between two competitors. That level of sophistication may take longer to develop. Initially, there will be a very patchy response.

THE NATURE OF THE COMPETITION

That is because the various competitors are so varied. Large public authority direct works departments will be competing with local small landscape construction contractors. Individuals seeking to set-up their own business will be tested alongside massive national (sometimes international) conglomerate companies. Some will have a local base, others will not.

Costings will therefore be very variable.

Fig. 5.1 The journey will become smoother

The variability of the companies tendering will settle down as the decade of the 1990s elapses. The earlier a company puts itself in the fray and competes, the better. Learn as you go, change as opportunities occur.

Curiously, the changes to the bus services (of all things) in the mid-1980s could be a portent for the future. Anyone can see the dramatic difference in bus services around the country since de-regulation. Some changes have been for the better, others for the worse. Many companies have changed hands. Furthermore, bus services have become much more regular, compared to the early days following the de-regulation in 1986. A similar stabilizing period will no doubt follow with grounds maintenance in the 1990s.

The final aspect affecting tendered costs is the availability of year-round work. It is indeed the crucial requirement of all landscape contractors. To take on seasonal staff is both time-consuming and wasteful. The staff built up during the summer leave in the autumn. All that effort for nothing, and the good ones never return!

WINTER, THE GREAT TIME LOSS

Even worse is the effort required to find work during the winter for the few remaining permanent staff. There is nothing more punishing for a business, than paying wages to under-employed staff. Winter wages can be a very high on-cost to a landscape contracting company. It is an example of lost time at its worst.

Winter is a time when the depot is tidied up, the nursery is sorted out and when a multitude of tasks are undertaken. Very theraputic, no doubt, but hardly cost-effective.

The work is not being costed to a job which pays money. And that is the key to any successful business.

Every job needs to pay more money than it costs. That is a fairly obvious point in order to make a profit, but so often it is overlooked; or rather, not considered.

The need for cleaning the depot, tidying the nursery, is itself too obvious to need explanation. That is accepted, but how long is it taking?

Usually it takes as long as the time available.

It would take much less time if the job were costed – like all other work. The cost of what is loosely called 'winter maintenance' is amazing. If accurately priced, it would be done in half the time, or less.

So what is the answer?

There is little point in completing the task in half the time – if for the rest of the time staff are sitting around doing absolutely nothing. That hits at morale.

There is only one answer: go and look for work. There are any number of worthwhile tasks to be undertaken during the winter, for which a client will pay. All those park benches could be brought inside, scrubbed down and repainted. Any local authority would willingly consider renovation of all its public signs during the winter.

Fig. 5.2　Winter jobs can pay too

Winter work

It is the standard of winter maintenance which sets a public park at a higher standard than its neighbours. Parks with high standards of maintenance get more attention and respect. So, winter maintenance can mean less vandalism and greater public appreciation of the park or playing-field.

Summer work leaves no time for fabric maintenance of signs, bins, seats, etc. During the summer all attention and manpower is placed on the essential seasonal tasks which horticulture demands. Winter provides the breathing-space. Such essential tasks as decorating park pavilions, edging the footpaths and re-staking young trees are ideal tasks for the winter.

The contractor will have the time available. It is in the client's interest to use that resource. A multitude of tasks can be undertaken which will be a credit both to the client and the contractor.

Unfortunately, too often these tasks are not carried out. Why? Simply because the client is tied up in his office making budget preparations for next year. Similarly, the contractor is too busy (he thinks) tidying up the depot and nursery.

The final word on year-round work: vary the hours of the working week.

ANNUAL WORKING AND VARIABLE HOURS

Blackpool landladies spend a month or more in Majorca in the off-season. No work for them then, but they work long and hard during the summer and autumn season. They, no doubt, deserve their own vacation and time off. But do not miss the simple point: their hours and payment vary according to the season. Longer hours per week in the summer, shorter hours in the winter.

Surely the same is true of horticulture? The 40-hour working week is a myth a second time over. It is virtually impossible to work a 40-hour, 5-day week during the winter in the UK. There just isn't sufficient daylight. With the new methods of working in the 1990s, those who succeed will be those who take time to rethink some basic facts of life.

SUMMARY

The key points in this chapter refer to organization; and particular emphasis has been placed on the need to address a number of inherently poor horticultural working practices. Furthermore, the importance of accurate assessment of hourly costs, and waging war on lost time, cannot be overstressed. Accuracy improves with practice; all competitors know that.

- Basic hourly rates must be calculated to include *all* costs, overheads and on-costs for travel, rest and personal needs.
- The 40-hour week is a myth; due allowance is needed for lost time.
- Everyone needs to take the responsibility to calculate his own personal lost time, no one else can.
- Everyone needs to wage war continually on lost time; each person's co-operation is needed.
- Time is money.
- The most cost-effective combination of machinery and men to undertake each task in the tender will need to be accurately assessed by each contractor.
- Estimating is then easy: accurately assess how long each task will take and multiply by the real hourly rate.
- Involve all staff at all times; that is always good for morale, it also ensures that everyone is then committed to delivering the service at the given price.
- Competitors will vary in size, and in prices submitted.
- Successful contractors will ensure that they do not become uncompetitive due to underemployment, especially in the winter.
- All time will need to be costed and allocated against actual income-generating tasks.
- Look for winter work.
- Suggestions to clients for winter work need to be considered.
- Winter work may include painting park pavilions or refurbishing signs or park benches.
- That would greatly improve appearances, together with the public's respect.
- Winter work is of real value both to the client and the contractor.
- Very competitive prices can be offered by the contractor in the winter due to the lack of other income-generating activity.
- The client can use any unexpected savings which have accrued during the year (there always are some) to create a real improvement to the parks.
- Finally, what reason can there be for working a 40-hour week summer and winter?
- Variable hours between the peak and off-peak season must make more sense.

The success of a contractor (in the public or private sector) will be largely determined by his ability profitably to balance time and costs. It is an equation which goes to the very heart of every tender submission. Furthermore, it is an equation which will need daily reckoning.

ADDENDUM: THE COST OF LOST TIME

The details in this addendum are reproduced with permission of Colin Raynor, Public Sector Services, a consultancy specializing in competitive tendering.

It provides a carefully worked example of lost time incurred due to travel (walking) and an allowance for holidays and expected time off due to illness. By eliminating slackness, by means of a weekly log, a reduction in manpower and cost is possible. 'Hours bought' relates to the hours paid by the employer. 'Hours sold' relates to the actual real working hours (i.e. less lost time) which are sold to the client. Hours sold are obviously much less than the 39 hours bought per week. How much less, depends upon the working practices of each team.

PRESENT METHOD
LOST TIME

DAILY:		MINS	WEEKLY
	WALK TO BREAK	20	100
	WALK FROM BREAK	20	100
	WALK TO LUNCH	20	100
	WALK FROM LUNCH	20	100

WEEKLY = CASH CHEQUE   30   30

TOTAL 430

42 WORKING WEEKS PER YEAR **18060** ÷ 60 = 301 HRS

TIME LOST PER PERSON PER ANNUM =   **301** HRS
LEGITIMATE TIME LOST PER PERSON =   **406** HRS

707

PRESENT METHOD HOURS SOLD = **2028** - 707 = 1327 HRS

HOURS BOUGHT
HOURS SOLD

HOURS BOUGHT

16 X MEN X 8 HRS. X 4 =   512
16 X MEN X 7 HRS X 1 =   112
TOTAL 624

HOURS LOST

16 X TEA BREAK EXCESS OF 30 MIN WALKING PER DAY   40
16 X LUNCH BREAK EXCESS OF 30 MIN WALKING PER DAY   40
16 X BONUS SHEET RECKONING 1 HR. PER WEEK   16
16 X CASHING PAY CHEQUE 30 MIN PER WEEK   8
TOTAL 104

ACTUAL HOURS SOLD

16 X MEN =   PER WEEK   TOTAL 520

ERADICATE THE SLACKNESS

THE PEOPLE EFFORT IN MAN HOURS PER WEEK IS

$$520 \div 39 = 13 \cdot 33 \, MEN$$

EXAMPLE
SUPERVISOR'S LOG

NAME _____

No OF MEN IN GANG _____ *10* _____

WEEK COMMENCING _____

	HRS. BOUGHT	HRS SOLD	PLUS	MINUS
MON	80	72		8
TUE	72	63		9
WED	80	76		4
THU	80	80	—	—
FRI	64	62		2
SAT	—	—	—	
SUN	—	—		
TOTAL	376	353	NIL	23

NAMES _____

LEAVE: ___SMITH ON LEAVE ON TUESDAY___

SICK: ___JONES AND WILLIS SICK___

ABSENT: _____

SUPERVISOR'S LOG

NAME _____

No OF MEN IN GANG _____

WEEK COMMENCING _____

	HRS BOUGHT	HRS SOLD	PLUS	MINUS
MON				
TUES				
WED				
THU				
FRI				
SAT				
SUN				
TOTALS				

NAMES: _____

LEAVE: _____

SICK: _____

ABSENT: _____

Chapter Six

Winning tenders

Winning a contract comes only at the end of a long, hard haul. A successful contractor will have often submitted many tenders, to a number of very different authorities, in his bid for successful selection.

Submitting the applications is the easy part of the task. Once credentials have been checked, and invitation lists prepared, the contractor then has the onerous task of completing the tender documents. Inevitably the size and complexity of grounds maintenance leads to large Bills of Quantity.

Each item has to be priced with absolute accuracy for the successful contractor subsequently to deliver the service – at a profit.

BILLS OF QUANTITY

It is this onerous task of completing the Bills of Quantity which can deter the otherwise dedicated contractor. Even public sector contractors flinch at the thought of completing another tender for yet another authority. They are often too exhausted having completed their own. This is a hurdle which has to be overcome. For a contractor to be successful in the long run needs dedication and commitment to completing a range of tenders.

Completing tenders becomes easier as the estimator becomes more experienced.

Any contractor completing one tender complains about the difficulty of the task (even if he is successful). After two or three tenders, he may feel very sore at the great differences between them. Tenders for apparently very similar types of work may differ totally in their format. This makes it impossible to transfer a set of prices worked out for one tender to another. The agony increases.

Long-distance runners, and joggers for that matter, are all too familiar with the 'pain barrier', the pain in the ribs which occurs within the first 10 minutes of commencing the run. In fact it is the body adjusting to the necessary oxygen levels.

The pain barrier also occurs in competitive tendering.

The work involved in the first tender submission is dreadful, and for the next three or four, the pain becomes even worse. Then comes the good news. Most estimators find things easier after half a dozen.

The common thread between the various tenders has become apparent.

ITEMIZED COSTING SCHEDULE

The next step taken by most contractors is to prepare an itemized list of estimated costs. This sets out in great detail the composition for all estimates. Estimates for grass cutting are meaningless – there are so many kinds of grass cutting: different machines have differing work output, different types of grass and sports surfaces have distinct cutting regimes and the frequency of cut often varies between authorities. So does the type of machine which is specified.

An estimate for grass cutting, then is valueless to a contractor, except for the one tender for which the specific estimate was prepared.

So an itemized list of estimates needs to be detailed. This pricing schedule may take many years to achieve; it will be built-up from a number of component parts:

- the hourly rate for gardeners;
- the hourly rate for supervisors;
- the hourly rate for a triple grass mower;
- the hourly rate for gang mowing;
- the cost of transporting men and machines, per mile;
- the estimated time to take to undertake a specific task (e.g. mow a bowling-green).

Given this type of information, estimating can be accomplished more quickly and easily. Preparation of such a list takes time and skill. This is where the acumen of the successful contractor comes to the fore. By building up a valid costing base, he will be in a position to be able to tender for many contracts.

The next major ingredient for success is local knowledge.

If a contractor has a good pricing schedule, and has a working knowledge of the contract area, then he is in a very strong position to win the tender. All he now needs is the skill necessary to combine the two. This comes from experience.

Some contractors submit applications for dozens of contracts in their bid to win work. This is only possible where the contractor has the necessary skill, expertise and background knowledge to ensure efficient completion of the contract documents. Again, it takes time and ability to achieve the necessary size to field this number of applications.

Many contractors fear that it is beyond them to achieve a wide spread of contracts. Even local authority in-house contractors tend to call it a day after securing their own contract. That is not necessarily a wise course of action, especially where tenders are annually competed for. Every contractor needs constant exposure to tendering continually to be successful: it is clear that contractors who are continually making tender submissions become increasingly successful.

It is the ability constantly to submit tenders every year which has, no doubt, led to the spectacular growth of a number of contractors.

CSG (BATH) LTD*

One such company is the Contractor Services Group (CSG), originally formed from the contractor elements within Bath City Council. From small beginnings, they have grown to become one of the biggest tenderers in the country within a remarkably short space of time. They have every intention of becoming a company operating on a country-wide scale in a number of different services, including cleaning and highways. In one year the Group managed to be placed on the tender lists of no less than 46 authorities.

Subsequently they achieved a fair geographic spread of contracts. Initially, these were in the southern half of the country, stretching from London to Cornwall. This enabled the Group to extend its area of operation in such a manner to help its future expansion.

'This is our "lily pad" policy', explained Chris Jenkyn, Group Chairman and Chief Executive. 'Winning contracts in a number of

Fig. 6.1 A 'lily-pad' policy

*Author's Note: page 104.

separate locations provides us with working bases. This allows us to gain a good view of that particular part of the country. Our intention is then to use this base, or 'lily pad', to achieve a leapfrog in subsequent years.'

The Group is also quite happy at achieving second place in any tender situation.

If the lowest tenderer fails to commence the contract for any reason, then Contractor Services (CSG) are well placed. By submitting applications for dozens of tenders, they have won a fair number.

The Group have achieved a market penetration equalled by few. Their success has been equal to their commitment. Chris Jenkyn continued:

'We have declined invitations, as well. We are not in the business of entering tenders regardless of the conditions. Some of the conditions are manifestly unfair.'

He refers especially to high-performance bonds and personal liability clauses, not that the Group challenges such practices. Its task is to submit tenders, to be successful and to subsequently deliver the service. Their time and effort is entirely devoted to those ends:

'We have developed a positive and prudent approach to our expansion. It is by careful judgement that we have achieved our current position. We aim to build steadily.

Also, our business is about people. We are not an us-and-them company. Everyone is involved. All employees are shareholders. Also the General, Municipal and Boilermakers' Union are a shareholder in the company and have a place on the Board. This is a very evident aspect of our company status, and it is good for fostering local authority goodwill.'

The total approach by CSG confirms the care and attention given to all the details necessary for success in this very specific market-place. They believe that they enjoy a particular advantage in submitting tenders, and operating contracts, due to their local council background. All members of management of the Group know and understand the requirements of their various clients. Furthermore, they build on this strength by usually employing staff direct from the authority where a contract is to be operated. This helps to ensure a real cohesiveness within the wider Group.

They have also found that their origins have provided sufficient confidence to financiers; Chris Jenkyn explained:

'We kept well clear of venture capital companies. We could never afford their interest rates. This was achieved by ensuring we had no substantial purchase of capital assets. We could never hope to service a debt which required returns of 20%, or more. Local authority services will never be that profitable.'

So the Group has limited itself to maintaining sufficient liquid financial assets as is necessary to allow the contracts to function smoothly.

Their local government background, however, has not shielded CSG from confrontation with some prospective clients. Indeed, in some cases, it may have led directly to difficulties. Some local authorities see groups like CSG as predators, reneging on their historic ties with local government.

Whether for this reason or genuine contract validation purpose, the group have been subject to intense scrutiny by many clients. One authority went to the expense of sending a team of six of their officers to the headquaters of the Group to complete the investigations. This team took two days satisfying themselves about the Group. In the end, CSG and the authority did not enter into a contract.

Another authority where there was close competition required the Group to go to the expense of re-tendering. Amazingly, on receipt of the second lot of tenders, that authority called in consultants to help evaluate the submissions. Both submissions (i.e. the Group submission and that of the in-house direct services organization) were well beyond the budget provision which the council had made.

Of course, expense and time had been incurred by the Group in their submissions. This type of difficulty and frustration is common to all contractors. It is a real frustration, endemic in tendering.

That applies to existing direct works contractors, even when operating from within a local authority. A situation was reported in London where an attempt was made to settle old scores during the tender exercise. A local authority committee recommended that a grounds maintenance contract should not be awarded to the in-house contractor, despite the fact that it was the lowest bid.

Of course, if the committee had such serious reservations, then that in-house contractor should not have been invited to tender in the first place. Similarly, many of the other difficulties which surface at tender submission could have been anticipated and avoided.

However, the practice of tendering is far from perfect. Until it is perfected more, this kind of frustration and difficulty will continue.

The practice of tendering can be compared to a hurdle race. The only difference is that, with tendering, a tenderer is never able to see just how many hurdles there are on the track. New hurdles seem to appear from nowhere. It would surprise many contractors to learn that many a client also fails to foresee all the hurdles.

CDC LANDSCAPES

One company which has experienced perhaps less difficulty than most is the Suffolk-based contractor CDC, a part of the CDC Group of companies, with widespread interests. They have operated a number of traditional grass cutting contracts in the past for government ministries and similar bodies, both in the UK and on the continent.

With the diversity involved in the new grounds maintenance contracts, the company took an early decision to try to stay near home. Within their first year they were successful in winning the contracts in three neighbouring authorities in Essex. This provided them with a solid base.

As with many of the earlier tenders, the work involved was principally grounds maintenance. Although a number of small parks were included, there was no requirement to look after aviaries, or the like. Again, this company submitted many applications. That was necessary to achieve their objective of securing work in adjacent areas.

The company also won a contract in Hampshire, with the Area Health Authority. Although many miles from their main base, it was adjacent to a company branch. More important, that contract complemented work already being undertaken in the vicinity.

SUMMARY

Here the more important experiences mentioned in this chapter are highlighted, as follows:

- Submitting tenders is a long, time-consuming and difficult process.
- Tenders for apparently similar types of work vary one from another.
- Initially, this makes the task of submitting tenders more onerous.
- Once an estimator has become experienced in tender submissions, multiple applications are easier.
- A pricing schedule, based on component parts, is of great assistance in estimating.
- However, the preparation for each tender still requires much work and commitment.
- Local knowledge is essential for success.
- Some contractors submit dozens of tender applications.
- They hope to achieve successful submissions in approximately up to half a dozen. This can be a costly and high risk policy.
- Some contractors submit for only one tender.
- This is especially true of the in-house public authority contractor.

- This too can be a high-risk policy.
- Annual practice at tender submission is needed to, at least, keep in touch with the competitive environment and current prices.
- Some in-house contractors specialize in bidding successfully for tenders in neighbouring authority areas.
- Some contractors who have their origins in local authorities are now undertaking contract work throughout the country.
- The Contractor Services Group, based in Bath, is one such contractor.
- Their determination to succeed has managed to overcome all the usual (and some unusual) hurdles in tender submissions.
- The only difference between the practice of tendering and a hurdle race is that in the latter, all the hurdles can be seen.

The successful bids appear to come from contractors who have climbed the 'learning curve', and furthermore, those who have a definite policy towards the type (and location) of contract that best suits them. Those contractors then rigorously search for opportunities to implement that policy, as little as possible is left to chance.

This is equally true of contractors in the public sector as the private sector. Always there is a danger in any contractor accepting merely the current workload, not seeking extra work.

ADDENDUM: CHECK-LIST FOR COMMENCING A CONTRACT

1. After submitting the tender, seek written quotations (or tenders) for all plant, vehicles, machinery and equipment supplies.
2. Consider leasing as well as purchase.
3. Require fixed prices and delivery dates.
4. Draft a schedule of work i.e. the specific manner in which the workload will be tackled.
5. List manpower, teams, machines, routes – all as envisaged in the tender submission.
6. Negotiate with the client, if necessary, about any possible contract cuts.
7. State the commissioning period required, allow sufficient time for setting up.
8. Recruit staff, paying particular attention to the need for skilled contract supervisors.
9. All managers and supervisors need to walk the sites and all scheduled work routes.
10. Draft, on a weekly basis, all documents to operate and monitor the contract profitably.

11. Agree with the client work programmes and weekly schedules.
12. Finalize the formalities e.g. financial bond, insurance and indemnities.
13. Arrange dress rehearsals for supervisors, including dummy orders and schedules. Make returns, calculate profit and identify practical difficulties.
14. Take delivery of all supplies, equipment, plant, vehicles and machinery.
15. Hold briefings for all chargehands and teams.

Author's Note: CSG (Bath) LTD. Since writing this chapter, CSG (Bath) Ltd, have ceased operating. This was the result of a difficult trading situation. All the comments however remain valid and stand testimony to the company. Obviously, the high risk nature of tendering is emphasized by this example.

Chapter Seven

Performance indicators

There is no point in a contractor winning a tender if he cannot subsequently deliver the goods. Performance is a critical feature of all contracts. More important, performance monitoring will be a critical feature for every client authority and every contractor.

The contractor will have an overriding interest in profit, the client in service standards. But in a healthy situation, both the contractor and the client will have totally intermixed interests in the success of the entire contract.

Invariably, where a contract has turned sour, it has been due to lack of performance by the contractor; however, it has also often been due to lack of performance monitoring by the client. A failed contract means failure on both sides.

CLIENT INSPECTION

A contractor just does not suddenly 'go bad'. Often, as with poor workmanship, the situation slowly gets worse and worse. The critical issue is that the client has not adequately monitored the contract and required the contractor to repeat unsatisfactory work.

The standard of client inspection (and subsequent action) will vary radically from area to area. Sometimes contractors will get away with it – until the lack of maintenance results in a crisis. Only then is client action taken. This is far too late and everyone suffers (client, contractor and the public).

The contractor should never rely on the client inspection procedure to rectify his mistakes.

Indeed a good client will rectify poor performance by a contractor, but there is a catch: it will be rectified (quite rightly) at the contractor's expense. Appropriate deductions will be made, and payments will be delayed, while the issue is sorted out. Thus any contractor will quickly be brought to heel.

The contractor therefore needs to develop systems of monitoring performance. These will go far beyond merely responding to client complaints.

PROFIT

A contractor is critically interested in profit. Performance measures will start with profit, and finish with profit. Because if there is no profit, then there is a loss. It does not take long for a loss to turn into a contractor going bankrupt and the workforce being made redundant.

Even within the public sector, the in-house teams are required to make a profit. At least 5% return on capital is required by the secretary of state. Those in-house contractors with multiple depots spread around the district carry a huge burden. This is further added to with an expensive fleet of vehicles.

Great attention must be paid to that 5% by public sector contractors. The actual current valuation of the depots will be of critical attention.

Public sector profit

The 5% requirement will be particularly biting on the depots and fleets or vehicles; the government require a 5% return on the current value of such assets. The emphasis is placed on current value. Often many contractors in the private sector will operate from long-established (and long since paid for) depots. The public sector's assets however will be regularly re-valued. The public sector contractor has therefore the same need to make a profit year by year just to stay in business. If any public sector contractor fails in this requirement, he will be closed down eventually.

Before concentrating on profit, there is another fact of life that must be taken into account by contractors. That is the penalty to be paid for defaults.

A default in an important and sensitive area will provoke a greater reaction than many defaults in less critical areas (e.g. a bowling-green compared with many smaller minor areas of grass around the town).

Default

Let the bowling-green be unprepared for a weekend match and everyone will know about it. Should it be a county match which is affected, or worse, the President's Annual Championship Day, then the hue-and-cry needs to be heard to be believed.

The mayor and press will be the least of the Contractor's worries. Payments will be withheld; time will be wasted while the witch-hunt is undertaken; and the full penalties of the contract will be enforced. And all due to a lack of sensitivity on the part of the contractor. He can only blame himself.

So an ear to the ground, and an eye to the accounts, will be the motto of the successful contractor.

It is a basic and simple statement of fact that all businesses succeed by turning in a profit, year by year. However, there is often a lack of understanding among many businesses as to what their particular profit constitutes.

Annual gross profit

To many, it is the surplus after all the wages have been paid. At best, this could be called gross profit as, of course, all the costs of vehicles, plant, debt charges, etc. still have to be met. All these costs would be taken out of the gross profits before a net profit can be obtained.

Others just accept what the accountant says at the end of the year. He must be right!

But what good is an accountant's figure at year end? It is a bit late then to make changes.

Limited value

And often it takes the accountant many a month to prepare the accounts. Any change which is undertaken due to concerns generated by the annual accounts will only take effect well into the second year.

Fig. 7.1 Annual accounts are too late for action

The full effects of any change then would only be seen in the third year.

A much more immediate assessment of profit is needed by the contractor. Moreover, maintenance is different from landscape construction, which has often been the staple diet of landscape gardening companies.

Maintenance contracts are big: work up to £1 million can comprise just 20% of a large metropolitan area. Smaller contracts will be the norm in towns and districts. However, even a contract of £100 000 – lasting all the year – will be a small yet equally difficult contract, and will need constant and careful monitoring.

ASSESSMENT

Furthermore, no matter how big or small the total contract, control and profitability will only be established on the ground by each team, each day of each week. A simple profitability measure is therefore required.

For the student of efficiency, there are any number of ratios which may be applicable. Today Key Performance Indicators abound in academic study. A ratio, or indicator suitable for each specific and particular area of work, is the only one to be recommended.

Assessment of each team

To find the most appropriate indicator requires assessment of the business in which it will be used. Like it or not, grounds maintenance is but a fragmented business. There are many small business units (or working teams) scattered across many square miles of a district. Each unit (or team) needs to be able to assess its own profit situation, daily and weekly. In this aspect, at least, there is little difference with big business.

Models

National (or international) conglomerate companies make their profit from tens (or even hundreds) of small companies dotted all over the country. Perhaps they have a model to copy. In essence, the Head Office, wherever it may be, is only interested in the profit turned in by each unit.

This has to be a method for careful study.

Assessment: an example

Small businesses are increasingly taking their cue from big business. Look at hotels: within most hotels there are a number of separate

Fig. 7.2   The grocer keeps weekly records

specialist teams. They provide for catering, banqueting, conferences, reception, cleaning, bookings, services, etc. Often these separate functions are run as separate entities. They are operated as separate cost/profit centres.

The Conference side of the hotel will agree a menu from the catering side, then pay the price agreed with the caterers. Each separate function within the hotel will run its own profit-and-loss account.

The same is true of even smaller businesses. Take a look at a local shop: every shopkeeper knows whether he is up or down on his takings in any week, compared to that same week last year. He will also know exactly the percentage mark-up he makes on all his stock. The mark-up will be less for staple goods like bread and milk – (it could be even less than 10%). For luxuries, the mark up will increase to 40%, or more depending on the item.

SALE PRICE

The shopkeeper takes as his base the price he has to pay the wholesaler. The retailer's percentage mark-up is then his best judgement as to the price that he can sell the most goods for while, at the same time, achieving an adequate profit.

Grounds maintenance contractors will succeed using the same indicators as all businesses, big and small.

To have been successful in winning the contract in the first place, the contractor will have committed himself to a given price for a given amount of work.

Say £100 has been quoted for planting out a bedding-plant display, 100 m in size. The contractor will, no doubt, have carefully calculated the £100 – and it will have included all costs incurred (wages, plant, vehicles, on-costs, an element for profit, the 5% return, etc.).

COST PRICE

To be successful, the work must be carried out for no more than £100; or better still, for less than £100. Only constant monitoring by the teams on the ground will ensure that each and every cost is kept to.

Where an approved nominated subcontractor is used, his rate will have to be no higher than, say, £95: no danger here of overpaying on the tendered price. But subcontracting will be allowed only on a small percentage of the total contract. Otherwise the client authority would have employed the subcontractor in the first place, benefiting by the cheaper price. However, the same business principles apply. The main contractor still gains 5% (or £5 if the subcontractor quoted and agreed £95).

PROFITABLE SUBCONTRACTING

As the shopkeeper adds a percentage to gain his profit margin, so must the ground maintenance contractor. The Conference Manager of a large hotel buys his meals from the Catering Manager but still adds his own 5% profit margin (or more). Again, the same principles apply to grounds maintenance.

Returning to the example of big business, grounds maintenance is not that much different. Change the words 'shop floor' to 'ground floor' and the similarity is evident for all to see.

The starting-point for profit calculation has to be the tendered price. That, or better, must be achieved. Each team within the contracting company will be judged successful or not on their ability to meet the tendered price. There is no easier way; indeed there is no other way.

Each job has to be undertaken at the tendered cost or less. Perhaps each team should have the opportunity to help in fixing the price in the first place, especially as their future will depend on it.

The mass of individual tasks which go to make up most grounds maintenance contracts would seem to make it impossible to try to keep control of costs by checking each job. Near-impossible it may prove to be, but how else can the difference between profit and loss be ensured?

The entire computer industry has grown up (and is still growing) on the task of providing exact and accurate job costing.

People divide into two groups in their attitude to computers: there are those who believe that computers never work, never do what they promised to do at the outset, and when they do, actually produce only what is wrong: the other category are the believers. These may believe that the advance of computers are the twentieth-century equivalent of the cavalry charge – sweeping all before them – and the only difference being that computers are safer.

COMPUTERS AND MANUAL SYSTEMS

Well, perhaps, the truth lies somewhere in between. Computers do have a lot to offer, even if not as much as the salesman would have everyone believe.

Computers are designed to crunch numbers, to absorb diverse bits of information and then give out meaningful reports on efficiency and effectiveness. Some examples of computer applications are given in the Addendum at the end of this chapter.

It is easy to be carried away on a wave of euphoria about computers and their applications – especially when on the receiving end of a sales drive. Yet computers can do only what they are told. Furthermore, whatever a computer does, can also be done manually – with a sheet of paper and a pencil. Indeed before committing any cash to a computer, it is well worth trying out the system – the Business Secretary is far from redundant yet!

Whether a computer or manual system, the main key to success will be to accurately predict the profit or loss on each job. Each team leader needs to take responsibility for his own team's profitability.

No competent company would send out a team of gardeners and groundsmen without motor mowers and hand tools. Yet how often is the principal tool of the trade missing? All the best plant and equipment is useless unless profitably used.

PROFIT FROM DIVERSITY

In this chapter we have concentrated on the element of profit in the contract. Achieving a profit from so many diverse individual tasks will be a new and onerous responsibility for the contractor, whether in the private or public sector.

Private landscape companies have in the past tended to operate on individual contracts (e.g. a construction project). The profit or loss on the one project is clearly evident. Not so in the future.

Profit or loss will be made in a vast number of different places of work, each and every day.

For the public sector, profit will be an unusual concept. Traditionally the public sector has been service-oriented, not profit-oriented. The nearest they have got to a conception of profit is by working a bonus system.

The standard minute values (SMVs) of an outdated bonus system will be a dangerous base for determining profit. Worse still, outdated SMVs will distort the analysis of tasks, to the very real detriment of any successful business venture.

The easiest way to fail in business is by not knowing what are the profitable activities and the unprofitable.

A shopkeeper knows his most profitable lines – and what products are sold at virtually cost price. Careful analysis of his sales allows him to achieve a profit. Nothing less is needed of the successful ground maintenance contractor.

SUMMARY

The key points in this chapter are the following:

- Failure only comes about due to lack of monitoring.
- If a contract is terminated, both the client and the contractor have failed.
- However, it is only the contractor who loses his business.
- Poor performance is always corrected at the contractor's expense.
- Both public and private sector contractors have to make a profit.
- In the public sector a minimum return is required of 5% on the current value of capital assets (buildings, plant, vehicles etc.).
- That means, to be successful, the tender must be the lowest on offer, yet still allow the works to be undertaken to allow a profit.
- A profit needs to be made on each activity – by each team, every day.
- Critical attention is therefore required to daily performance.
- Beware the highly sensitive areas where real skill is required (e.g. fine turf).
- Here high standards of performance are essential if complaints are to be avoided (and more important, if extra work is to be avoided).
- Withholding payments to the contractor is a very painful penalty.
- It is also totally justified where works have to be repeated due to a fault by the contractor's teams.

- Year-end profit is all-important.
- It comes too late, however, for meaningful action to be taken.
- Much more important is the weekly assessment of each team's profit.
- Beware of being snared into too much detail.
- A simple weekly system of profit per team should be easily possible.
- This will be based on the original tendered price for the week's work.
- Computers may be able to help.
- Manual systems can be equally good.
- A shopkeeper knows which lines sell at 20%, 30% and 40% mark-up.
- He also knows which lines have only a 1–5% mark-up.
- Grounds maintenance contractors will need the same information.
- Like retailing, grounds maintenance is keenly competitive.
- The best performance indicators are devised, or specially chosen for, each individual contract.

The greatest success in contracting is based on adequate controls of the profit-and-loss situation. This, in turn, demands sufficient attention to the day-to-day control of the business. The most successful businesses are developed on systems and procedures specifically suited to that particular business.

ADDENDUM: SOME COMPUTER APPLICATIONS

Reproduced in this addendum are some typical parts from a maintenance contract available from a specialist computing company. They combine to form an integrated method of costed control.

They are reproduced by permission of Aramis Computing Services Ltd.

HEADER	SUB-HEADER	GROUP	ELEMENT
15 Grassland			
	15 Amenity		
		05 Level Ground	
			05 Fine ornamental Lawn
			10 High Standard
			15 Medium Standard
			20 Housing Areas,Open Spaces
			25 Low Standard
		10 Banks	
			05 Fine Lawns
			10 Type II
			15 Type III
		15 Naturalised Bulbs in Level Ground	
			05 Type I
			10 General Areas
			15 Low Standard
		20 Naturalised Bulbs on Banks	
			05 Type I
			10 Type II
			15 Type III
		25 Edging	
			05 High Standard
			10 Medium Standard
			15 Low Standard
	20 Sports Turf		
		05 Cricket Outfield	
			05 Type I
			10 Type II
			15 Type III
		10 Cricket Square	
			05 Type I
			10 Type II
			15 Type III
		15 Cricket Wicket	05 Type I
			10 Type II
			15 Type III
		20 Football Pitch	
			05 Type I
			10 Type II
			15 Temporary Football Pitch
		25 Rugby Pitch	
			05 Type I
			10 Type II
			15 Type III
		30 Hockey Pitch	
			05 Type I
			10 Type II
			15 Type III

Maintenance Contract for Victoria Park, Cardiff

ITEM	DESCRIPTION	QUANTITY	UNIT	RATE	PRICE /OCC	FREQ	ANNUAL PRICE
	VICTORIA PARK --------------						
	SOUTHERN ENTRANCE AND LAKE AREA -------------------------------						
	Inventory Unit 005/05/05 SOUTHERN GRASSED AREA						
0001	Collect litter and debris.	140	m2			12	
0002	As above	1538	m2			52	
0003	Remove leaves and other debris.	140	m2			1	
0004	As above	7	m2			2	
0005	Irrigate.	7	m2			5	
0006	Apply fertiliser.	7	m2			1	
0007	Keep area 98-100% free of weed cover.	1	m2			1	
0008	Hoe and weed.	7	m2			12	
0009	Keep grass height between 20-50mm.	1351	m2			1	
0010	Keep grass height between 35-75mm and remove arisings.	180	m2			1	
0011	Cut grass to 35mm and remove arisings.	180	m2			1	
0012	Cut grass to 50mm.	139	m2			2	
0013	Lift.	7	m2			2	
0014	Dead head.	7	m2			6	
0015	Maintenance prune.	140	m2			1	
0016	Tie-in.	7	m2			3	
0017	Fork over to 150mm depth and incorporate leaf litter.	7	m2			1	
0018	Carry out final preparation for planting.	7	m2			2	

| 001

ITEM	DESCRIPTION	QUANTITY	UNIT	RATE	PRICE /OCC	FREQ	ANNUAL PRICE
0223	Refill water feature for summer.	1	nr			1	
0224	Maintain in a serviceable condition.	2	nr			1	
0225	Paint.	154	m			1	
0226	Switch on.	1	nr			300	
0227	Switch off.	1	nr			300	
	Inventory Unit 005/05/75 PLAY GROUND TO SOUTH EAST OF PADDLING POND						
0228	Inspect condition and report to Landscape Manager.	5	nr			52	
0229	Carry out scheduled survey of play equipment and report to Landscape Manager.	5	nr			12	
0230	Rake loose material and remove litter and debris.	348	m2			52	
0231	Top dress with bark mulch.	348	m2			2	
0232	Keep area 100% free of weed cover.	348	m2			1	
0233	Maintain in a serviceable condition.	5	nr			1	
	Inventory Unit 005/05/80 ANNUAL BEDDING ADJACENT TO THE SE ENTRANCE GATE						
0234	Collect litter and debris.	29	m2			52	
0235	Remove leaves and other debris.	29	m2			2	
0236	Irrigate.	29	m2			5	
0237	Apply fertiliser.	29	m2			1	
0238	Hoe and weed.	29	m2			12	
0239	Lift.	29	m2			2	
0240	Dead head.	29	m2			6	
0241	Tie-in.	29	m2			3	

| TOTAL FOR PAGE 13 | | | C/f to Grand Summary | |

	TEMPORARY SPORTS AREA						

	Inventory Unit 005/20/05						
	GRASS						
0358	Collect litter and debris.	9254	m2			52	
0359	Keep grass height between 20-50mm.	9254	m2			1	
	Inventory Unit 005/20/10						
	FOOTBALL PITCH						
0360	Apply Spring and Summer fertiliser.	3684	m2			1	
0361	Apply Autumn fertiliser.	3684	m2			1	
0362	Keep grass height between 20-50mm.	3684	m2			1	
0363	Spike.	3684	m2			2	
0364	Roll.	3684	m2			1	
0365	Mark out and maintain markings.	480	m			1	
0366	Erect goal posts.	2	nr			1	
0367	Dismantle goal posts.	2	nr			1	
0368	Paint goal posts.	2	nr			1	
0369	Repair goalposts.	2	nr			1	

TOTAL FOR PAGE 23	C/f to Grand Summary

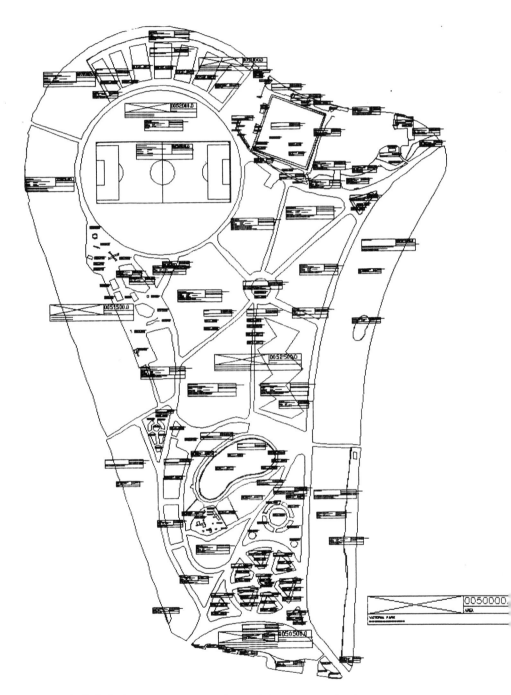

A digital plan to accompany the maintenance contract.

Chapter Eight

The winning bid

Any winner feels euphoria, the same is true of the winner of a tender. After all the hard work filling in forms, being scrutinized from every angle, the nail-biting tension of getting each and every bit right, euphoria should be the least of it.

But, by contrast, the actual announcement of the winner will be somewhat subdued, no civic announcement by the mayor from the balcony of the Town Hall, no red carpet.

The first that the winning tenderer will hear is, perhaps, a cautious phone call. It will be from the client officer for the local authority offering the tender. At this stage, the tenderer will not yet be the contractor – a subtle, but all-important, difference. There is good reason for that caution.

ERRORS

All too often the lowest tender is wrong. Unbelievably, if often contains errors. Simple arithmetical errors still occur. This is despite all the care and attention put in by the estimator when compiling the tender.

So what is to be done if the lowest tender contains an error?

From the client's point of view, it is a very difficult situation. Do you accept the tender, with the ever-present fear that the successful tenderer may then go bankrupt because his prices are too low? Or do you refuse the tender and risk the accusation of being anti-competitive?

THE NEXT-TO-LOWEST TENDER

Before answering that, it would be helpful to go back to that phone call. Caution is the byword. The person making the call knows everything; he knows the highest tender, the lowest tender – and all the prices in between. He is not likely to mention any of this on the phone, however.

Most important, he is acutely aware of the value of the next-to-lowest tender. The summary given in Table 8.1 tells all. Unfortunately, it may be all too familiar.

Table 8.1   Comparison of tender bids

Contractor Company/public authority	Tender bid (£)
A	450 000.00
B	246 012.67
C	392 467.00
D	437 787.92
E	612 413.23
F	421 043.76

Notes:
1. The difference between the lowest bid and the highest is more than 100%, a not uncommon occurrence. What does this say about the contractor with the highest bid? Is it likely that the client will invite that company to bid in future?
2. Most of the contractors seem broadly to agree about the value of the contract. They have bid between £390 000 and £450 000.
3. There is a difference of £150 000 between the lowest and the second lowest. So is the lowest tender to be trusted? The second lowest feels about right. It is near the majority of the others.
4. With compulsory competitive tendering, there will most often be only three or four bids to be considered. The disparity between the various bids could therefore be more striking.

Following that cautions phone call, the lowest tenderer will, no doubt, be called to the clients office for a discussion.

Never forget, the client knows all, and tells no-one.

INTERVIEWS AND SCRUTINY

Post-tender negotiations can be traumatic. Some contractors are totally unprepared. They assume, perhaps with some justification – that all the hard work and tension up to the point of submitting the tender is more than sufficient input by them.

However, given a variety of bids as illustrated in Table 8.1, it is only sensible for the client to undertake meticulous scrutiny.

The client is now talking to a prospective contractor. This contractor is to be entrusted with all the grounds maintenance operations in a proportion of the district for at least three years. The years of experience of complaints which the client will have had, and requests from the public, will sit heavily on his shoulders. If the client gets it wrong now, he will suffer heavily in the years to come.

The principal question the client will need answering is how and why the price is so low. Careful scrutiny will be made of the lowest prices contained within the tender.

For example, the lowest price contained in the tender was for hedge cutting. The client will want to know how the contractor intends to cut the hedge. A side-mounted tractor flail mower may be acceptable for highway roadsides but clearly would be unacceptable behind private gardens. The competitors may have priced for a more conventional method of working such as using hedge trimmers.

If the client did not specify that hedge trimmers were to be used, he may face a dilemma. He can hardly reject the tender because the contractor has used the cheapest method of operation. However, if it is physically impossible to drive a tractor near to back garden hedges, then obviously the price cannot be accepted.

Similarly, it will be quite acceptable to use a triple mower for much of the grass cutting. The client will be more than concerned if the triple mower price has been used to cost for the bowling-greens. That, at the very least, reveals totally insufficient attention to detail within the tender document; at worst, it indicates a total lack of competence.

The interview will be thorough. The client already knows much about the contractor from the appraisals. The technical/work competence and financial references will have established the basic credentials of the contractor. The site visits, prior to tender, will also have influenced the client's assessment of the contractor.

But at this stage of the process, those references are now history. They served their purpose at the time, indeed they were essential; but they do not provide the amount of detail now required.

The basis of a good marriage cannot be built on a chat with the friends of the intended. So the interview may well extend to more interviews, more site visits, and more scrutiny. This will be especially critical when there is only a slight difference between the lowest tender and the second lowest. Obviously the client is keen to get the best deal. Furthermore, at this stage, he will not mention price. The contractor is kept in the dark, while the client operates in a state of complete information.

There is another aspect of the total tender price which might give cause for concern to the client. Put simply, it may be more than he can afford.

TENDERS AND AFFORDABILITY

At the outset, the client will have estimated approximately how much the tender is worth. This cost will be met by those paying the local community charge ('poll tax') or by others (e.g. sports players),

Fig. 8.1   More than he can afford...

depending on the type of client authority. This estimate may have been £300 000. If the lowest tender happened to be £400 000, the client has a problem.

Some client authorities will be prepared to increase the community charge to provide the given level of service or provision. Others will not. How the interview progresses will depend on the type of authority, and its willingness to consider an increase. The sum of £100 000 is not much in tender terms, given the wide disparity of tender prices typically encountered. But it is, of course, a huge amount to find from an already hard-pressed budget.

CONTRACTOR QUESTIONING

It is an important time for a frank exchange of views about the inevitable additional works which will be required during the year. An acknowledged and open relationship, in these matters, is helpful to both parties. If a client is already in financial difficulty on opening the tenders, he is bound to become seriously embarrassed, long before the end of the financial year.

The contractor needs to lead the discussion. The line of questioning needs to establish whether the client has thought about the need for additional expenditure (for all the one-off jobs), and moreover, whether he has made budget provision. Next, the contractor needs to know if he will be given the first opportunity to price works of this nature. However, if the total price is causing the client concern, he needs to be open about it.

The number of options available to the client are few; but more important, they are clear-cut. First, the client can accept the tendered price and face the consequences of the increased cost. If this is not possible, then the client can stay with his estimate and seek reductions from the successful contractor. This will mean cutting the level of service.

Cuts

For the contractor, it will mean a lower total quantity of work, and thus income. The actual items to be omitted will need joint agreement, as will any proposed reduction in frequencies for any particular task. The actual areas of work to be cut out will be damaging to both the client and contractor. The reductions will need to be carefully assessed by both.

The client will not wish to see an unacceptable reduction in standards in those areas of work which are most in the public eye, or which may attract a violent backlash of complaints. Equally, the contractor will not wish to see his most profitable work pared off. Nor will he wish to be left with an unbalanced workload, unsuited to his methods of working.

Negotiation

Discussions, negotiations and a frank exchange of views will be the only way to resolve a difficult issue such as a reduction in the total tender value.

The client may also be talking to other contractors, especially if they were close in price to the lowest tender. He needs to do that, in case agreement with the lowest tenderer cannot be achieved. He should be honest enough to admit that he is involved in such discussions – if asked. Many contractors never ask. They think it is against the rules to ask such questions. Wrong. The more open the dialogue, the better for both parties. However, it needs to acknowledged that the lowest tender will invariably win.

Tension and delays

Honesty and openness is most important throughout the many discussions and interviews. At no time is it more vital to be honest and open than in the post-tender situation. This is the foundation point of a relationship to last three to six years. It is a tragedy if emotion or upset should cloud the start of such a crucial long-term relationship. Unless care and tact are employed by both sides, difficulties can set in before the contract even starts. Some contractors have found the post-tender negotiations the hardest.

There are two main reasons for that. First, the negotiations were unexpected. Second, the nature of the discussions appears, at times, to undercut the very essence of the tender submitted.

It is always reassuring to know that the interviews and negotiations will eventually come to an end. Furthermore, many contractors have had similar experiences. As time is limited for the client, and contractor, the interviews cannot be too protracted.

Once offered and accepted, the contract then has to wait for the legal formalities. Many people accuse lawyers of making mountains out of molehills. Well, they do – but for a very good reason. Their overriding objective is to protect their clients' interests. Any delays at this stage, although annoying, are all for their ultimate good.

The financial standing of the company will now come under the closest scrutiny. The financial performance bond will have to be paid – or more likely, the relevant insurance will have to be arranged. While all the office formalities are continuing the contractor needs all speed on the ground.

SETTING-UP FOR WORK

Prior to tender, the contractor will have sounded out the appropriate machinery and equipment suppliers. In view of the costs involved, competitive quotations will probably have been sought, or even competitive tenders. What is sauce for the goose is sauce for the gander. Of next importance to the price is the delivery date. There is no point in securing the best price if it means a delivery date long after the contract has started.

There will be a considerable shopping-list for machinery and plant. Some will be purchased, others hired and, perhaps, some provided on a leasing agreement. Financial advice is needed here, to secure the best terms.

Depots and work bases need to be established. Indeed all the ideas which went into preparing the tender bid in the first place now need to be actioned. This will involve much written detail. A successful contract runs smoothly only if everyone knows precisely what he should be

Fig. 8.2 Walk the site

doing, and when. Ultimately, the secret of success will be in managing such a diverse contract on a day-to-day basis.

Staff involvement

The importance of involving all personnel to be engaged in the contract cannot be overstated. This is particularly true of supervisory staff. Their function is the smooth running of the contract. They will not be in a position to manage unless they have walked the sites beforehand, and unless they have an intimate knowledge of the schedule of works for each team.

Preparation

So, while the office arrangements seem to drag on interminably, much work needs to be progressed on the ground, and orders placed with suppliers. Detailed working routes need to be closely planned with the men who will be delivering the service.

While all this preparation goes on, of course, the contractor is not being paid a penny from the contract. Payments will only commence after the contract has started, and that will be many weeks away.

In these circumstances, it is all too easy for the contractor to take the easy, short-term approach and fail to prepare adequately. Where a contract renewal is to take place, the temptation of short cuts is even greater. The greatest danger lies with those public sector contractors who are changing from the traditional parks department mode of working to a contractor method of operation.

Inertia is a deadly danger. Complacency kills.

Old methods of working cannot, and will not, be geared to a new contract. The only method in which to commence a new contract is with the completed specification, as priced by the contractor.

OPERATIONAL PLANS

In pricing the tender, the estimator will have in mind a method of working. That method may, or may not, have been written down. It is that method, and only that method, which can lead to successful operational achievement on the ground. In its turn, this demands attention to the manner in which the contract was priced in the first place.

An estimator working in an office on his own is bound to get it wrong. Everyone needs to be involved. The contractor manager, site supervisor, clerk of works, head gardeners, greenkeepers, all have their own specialism to bring to bear. It is their own expertise which will ensure success (or failure) in the contract situation. So it is important to include their input from the outset.

TRADE UNIONS

Also, of course, trade union representatives must be consulted and agreement reached. In the absence of trade unions, worker representatives are to be consulted.

It is then necessary to commit everything to paper. Methods of working, machinery, operational routes and task sequences need to be specified – and kept to by the maintenance teams. Simple! Simple it is, but all too often it is not carried out. This is especially true of an existing operator who, by default, carries on as in the past.

The ability to defend past operational methods is awe-inspiring. Yet it is misplaced. New methods must be based on the priced tender. The detailed methods for achieving this basic objective are the subject of Chapter 11.

SUMMARY

At this stage, it is important to exploit fully the time during which the legal formalities drag on. Having won the bid, a glass of champagne would be in order. But that should not give way to complacency. Many a contractor struggles to make a profit once a contract has commenced. All that can be avoided by wisely using the time now available.

As we have seen in this chapter, a winning bid may not be as straightforward as it first appears:

- No town crier ever announces that a contractor has won a tender.
- Instead a calm phone call will announce that a contractor is being considered for a formal contract.
- The caution of the client is based on knowledge which the contractor does not share.
- This may relate to very simple arithmetical errors, or a very close second lowest bid.
- The range of tendered prices often varies greatly.
- The highest bid may be as much as double the lowest.
- The client will therefore wish to discuss the details with the contractor, to satisfy himself that the contractor can deliver.
- All those pre-tender checks will again be gone through.
- Even greater emphasis is now placed on the financial and technical references.
- The financial bond will need to be secured.
- Some contractors find the post-tender period the most traumatic: success seems so near yet so far.
- Methods, machinery and prices will be scrutinized at meetings between client and contractor.
- The client will be comparing and contrasting with the other tenders and his own knowledge.
- Prices which appear especially low will be scrutinized all the more.
- These meetings are of real benefit to the contractor too.
- He needs to establish work schedules and routes in conjunction with the client.
- An open and honest relationship needs to be developed between the client and contractor.
- The start of the right relationship is vital.
- The contractor should press the client about the limit of his budget.
- Also about procedures to be adopted for the inevitable variation orders and one-off jobs.
- Eventually the contract will almost always be offered to the contractor with the lowest tendered price.

- Even then, there are seemingly endless delays while the legal formalities are settled.
- But all this time can be put to good use by the contractor in setting-up.
- Time and effort spent now will be recouped once the contract is operational.
- Inertia is a real enemy at this stage.
- There are so many good reasons why action should be delayed – not least the fact that payment will be made only when the contract commences.
- Machinery suppliers need to be alerted.
- Supervisors need to walk the many sites.
- For existing contractors (and parks departments), inertia may accompany complacency.
- Old working methods die hard.
- For a contract, the actual working methods need to be absolutely linked to the priced tender.
- If £20 has been quoted for mowing a bowling-green, the working methods will have to be linked to that price, and that task, to be successful.
- Provided the pricing was agreed with everyone before submission (supervisors, personnel and representatives, etc.), then there should be a good basis for a successful contract.

The time between a tender having been declared the lowest and the commencement of the contract is a time for intense activity. Close liaison with the client will commence; and frustration with the formalities will be an all too common occurrence.

A wise contractor will use this time to his maximum advantage. Especially important is the need to establish a good working relationship between client and contractor. Also it is essential to make full preparations for the execution of the contract on the ground, entirely in accordance with the detailed specification which has taken so long to price.

ADDENDUM: SOME BASIC SYSTEMS FOR CONTRACT CONTROL

The extracts presented here are reproduced from the Audit Commission publication, *Competitive Management of Parks and Green Spaces*, with permission of the Controller of Her Majesty's Stationery Office.

Exhibit 11

Components of a client computer system

A good computer system can manage the links between tasks, contracts, inspection and invoices

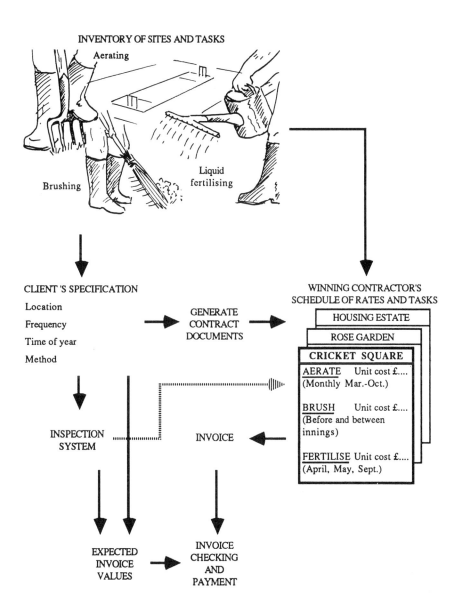

INVENTORY OF SITES AND TASKS

Aerating

Brushing

Liquid fertilising

CLIENT'S SPECIFICATION

Location
Frequency
Time of year
Method

GENERATE CONTRACT DOCUMENTS

WINNING CONTRACTOR'S SCHEDULE OF RATES AND TASKS

HOUSING ESTATE

ROSE GARDEN

CRICKET SQUARE

AERATE   Unit cost £....
(Monthly Mar.-Oct.)

BRUSH   Unit cost £....
(Before and between innings)

FERTILISE Unit cost £....
(April, May, Sept.)

INSPECTION SYSTEM

INVOICE

EXPECTED INVOICE VALUES

INVOICE CHECKING AND PAYMENT

Exhibit 13
Quality Assurance

In this system, client and contractor share the inspection burden

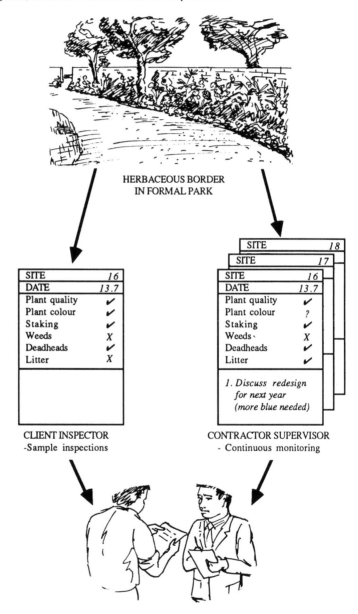

HERBACEOUS BORDER
IN FORMAL PARK

SITE	16
DATE	13.7
Plant quality	✔
Plant colour	✔
Staking	✔
Weeds	X
Deadheads	✔
Litter	X

CLIENT INSPECTOR
-Sample inspections

SITE	18
SITE	17
SITE	16
DATE	13.7
Plant quality	✔
Plant colour	?
Staking	✔
Weeds	X
Deadheads	✔
Litter	✔

1. Discuss redesign
for next year
(more blue needed)

CONTRACTOR SUPERVISOR
- Continuous monitoring

MEET AND DISCUSS

Exhibit 15

The variation in the time taken to do standard jobs in different authorities

There are wide variations in productivity. The ratio between the highest and lowest quarter of authorities is typically around 2:1

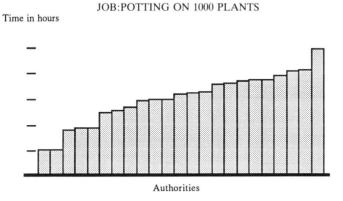

JOB:POTTING ON 1000 PLANTS

Time in hours

Authorities

Job	Ratio between times quoted by highest and lowest quarter of authorities	Job	Ratio between times quoted by highest and lowest quarter of authorities
Plants and shrubs		**Grass cutting**	
February rose bed pruning	1.71	Gang mowing	2.09
March shrub bed	2.23	Flail mowing	2.84
maintenance		Urban verges	4.05
Spring bedding	1.88	Parks grass	1.63
Make-up hanging baskets	1.60		
Nursery potting on	1.57	**Sports pitches**	
Nursery pricking out	1.71	Bowling green top dressing	2.90
Indoor floral displays	1.73	Bowling green morning	1.85
		maintenance	
Tree work		Post-match cricket wicket	3.95
Tree planting	1.81	renovation	
Tree maintenance	4.42	Pre-match football pitch	2.77
Tree felling	6.20	preparation	
		Autumn renovation of grass	3.04
		tennis court	

Source: Model jobs specified by Audit Commission and priced by local authorities

Chapter Nine

Contractor growth

All landscape contractors start in a small way, and if successful, grow larger.

TYLER ENVIRONMENTAL SERVICES

An excellent example is Tyler Environmental Services, one of the biggest local authority contractors in the country. Like everyone else, they started small and worked their way up. They are quick to seize opportunities as they occur. In that manner, they can adapt to changing business opportunities.

'The change to local government in London in 1965, really altered our approach to grounds maintenance', explained Mr Steward, Managing Director:

> We realized, at that time, there were many opportunities in London for contractors to undertake routine grounds maintenance operations. The new London boroughs were in many cases an amalgamation of smaller units and had difficulty sorting out their own internal arrangements. It made sense for many of the boroughs to employ outside contractors to undertake a proportion of the grounds maintenance works.

So Tylers began cutting grass verges, and the like, in a number of London boroughs. As a company, they found that they were particularly suited to carrying out some forms of grounds maintenance. They were able to maintain some areas more economically than the existing workforces of the borough:

> I believe that there is a place for both contract works and direct work in grounds maintenance. We both have our own specialisms, our strengths and our own weaknesses. A dual approach makes a lot of sense in many cases.

Over the years, Tylers have enlarged the range and type of work undertaken. One specific chance occurrence which arose in the early 1980s thrust the company into the very centre of the moulding force of competitive tendering.

VOLUNTARY TENDERING: LONDON BOROUGH OF WANDSWORTH

As a political decision, in the early 1980s, the London Borough of Wandsworth first sought tenders for a range of their grounds maintenance operations. Wandsworth led the drive to provide greater opportunities for private contractors. They believed that private contractors could do at least as good a job of work as the directly employed workforce. Furthermore, cost savings could also, perhaps, be achieved.

When tenders were opened, their beliefs in relation to reduced costs were seen to be amply justified. The borough awarded the contract to the lowest bidder, a company named Pritchards. This lowest-tender bid, was appreciably lower than the borough had expected (compared to their own estimates, as well as known costs from other private contractors).

Unfortunately, it was only in relation to price that the borough's expectations were found to be justified. Performance was, at best, poor.

Most local authority services have a high public profile, none more so than grounds maintenance. Given the political intention to succeed, and the added fact that the location was in the very centre of London, failure could not be countenanced. The contract was terminated.

This left the London Borough of Wandsworth with a problem. Now they had no one to undertake the grounds maintenance works.

Tylers were already working in nearby boroughs, and they offered to help. Their offer, of course, was based on their own rates and prices.

Not surprisingly, their offer was met with some resistance and scepticism. After some deliberation, their assistance was accepted, but only for a short period of time.

'We met a lot of antagonism', recalls Mr Steward:

> We were not the most welcome of visitors. The client officers of the borough were determined that a repeat of the last contract would not happen. However, they had a job they needed doing, and we had the resources to help.
>
> They watched our every move; and checked every single task we undertook. I am pleased to say that after helping out for a few weeks, we were offered a temporary extension.

This temporary arrangement continued until the council were able to seek formal tenders again.

Currently, Tylers undertake the grounds maintenance contract for the London Borough of Wandsworth, and a number of other London boroughs. Since the introduction of competitive tendering throughout the country, they have further increased the number of contracts which they operate:

> Over the years, I have more and more come to appreciate the importance of skilled operation of contracts. There is a real technique in running a highways grass cutting contract. Or at least, in running a grass cutting contract profitably.
>
> It's all about people. Our company is 100% about people. The supervisors, and all our employees are concerned about doing a good job. That way, we get invited back again, and more particularly, we get job satisfaction.

Tylers have also found it important over the years to keep good relations with local councillors and officers. Wounded feelings take a long time to heal.

TORBAY

Torbay, Devon, may not appear to have much in common with the London Borough of Wandsworth. However, in 1989, the local council in Torbay found itself in exactly the same situation that Wandsworth had found itself back in 1983. If uncut grass is unacceptable to an inner London borough, then it most certainly is totally unacceptable to a seaside resort. Furthermore, Torbay is a resort which takes great pride in matters of horticultural excellence.

A well-known and reputable national company were awarded the grass cutting contract in Torbay. It was some distance from their main centre of operations and a local subcontractor was appointed.

Unfortunately, the contract never properly commenced. Due to a number of difficulties (machinery, distance and communications), and the abilities of the contractors concerned, maintenance went from bad to worse. Quick action was required by the client.

Separate maintenance arrangements had to be made. Fortunately, the contract which had been let was for a small proportion of the total workload.

The client was able to call on the contractor who was undertaking other grounds maintenance works elsewhere in the district. This happened to be the authority's own in-house works organization. They were obviously competent, knowledgeable and able to take over. Not without some acrimony, however, as was to be expected. But making temporary arrangements is not the same as making permanent ones.

PERMANENT ARRANGEMENTS

To a large extent, in a contract situation, the client's hands are tied. The client has little option but to ask the second lowest tenderer. This tender is, of course, now the lowest. Or put another way, it is now the best value for money. Whether the second lowest tenderer is able to perform any more adequately than the first will not be known until the contract commences. Money has more importance in these matters than an assured standard of service delivery.

In the case at Torbay, the second lowest tenderer also happened to be the in-house contractor. So there was some cold comfort at the end of that particular saga.

This situation highlights the difficulty that both client and contractor face in a (tight) contractual situation. Total failure is almost as difficult as gradual deterioration.

The client approaches tendering from the viewpoint of service delivery. It is necessary to understand fully the standpoint of the client to appreciate the problems he faces.

The delivery of horticultural standards vary considerably between towns, and between towns and villages. Some authorities consistently provide a very high standard, some are indifferent and others are poor. That is a matter entirely for local pride. Some residents would prefer higher standards, others would prefer to pay less.

Consistency and continuity

The local authority has to decide the level of service which is to be provided, having taken account of local public opinion. The local

Fig. 9.1 Standards are consistent

authority then arranges for this work to be carried out to a consistent standard.

Whatever the level, they tend to be highly consistent. Such consistency has been guaranteed by the regularity of the authority's direct workforce.

This is always possible given a regular and stable workforce. Most of the staff remain from year to year. They know the work and work areas, and get on with it.

More important, the organization as a whole knows all the workload and the peculiarities of particular areas. So when one person retires or leaves the organization, there is no difficulty in covering the work. The average resident in the neighbourhood would see no difference in maintenance. The same is true if disciplinary action should lead to the dismissal of an employee. As far as the standard of service provided is concerned, there should be little change.

Collapse and maintenance

Maintenance by contract is totally different. When a contract is finished or terminated, it is not the same as one employee leaving. Everything changes. Even when the key personnel transfer to the new contractor, it takes a long time for maintenance standards to settle down again.

It is rather like cleaning out an ornamental pond. The task can be either accomplished by reducing the water level by, say, one-third, or if necessary, draining the pond altogether. If the pond has to be drained completely, then it will take months (and perhaps years) for the pond to regain its former state.

If a building contract is terminated, the building remains half-built until a new contractor is appointed. Such a solution is not possible with grounds maintenance. The grass does not stop growing.

Local authorities, will find themselves in totally new situation. By and large, it will not be a situation of their choosing; they will not like it. Local residents will not like it, and furthermore, they will not understand it.

It is into this situation that a number of contractors will have to venture. Examples have been given in the book of contractors from both the public and private sectors who have set about picking up the pieces. It is not easy. Immediate results are required, often in a hostile environment. The contractors (and clients) who adapt to this new regime quickly will be the most successful.

Non-maintenance of grounds will be an all too familiar occurrence with competitive tendering, whether due to contract termination or to a contract not commencing. Even at the start of the 1990s when compulsory competitive tendering formally commenced, contract defaults still occurred.

Unexpected opportunities

Clients and contractors will become increasingly familiar with dealing with this situation. It can be an unexpected opportunity to a contractor who is established and already known to a client. But any contractor needs to be able to produce exceptional performance if invited to help out.

The vast majority of contracts will, no doubt, be let and maintained in the normal manner, whether by the successful private or public sector contractor.

The start of the 1980s saw a high proportion of tenders being won by the local authorities themselves (about four out of five). Most authorities have totally changed their management arrangements to be more competitive. A number of contracts have been let to new companies, or companies expanding to fill this new market-place.

To try to accommodate the wishes of landscape contractors and the government, most authorities have let relatively small contracts. The average size of contract was about £250 000 at the start of the decade. This is much smaller than for all the other services subject to competitive tendering. With the average being £250 000, obviously much smaller contracts are being let.

Here there is considerably more scope than in most service operations.

There is much variety in the type, as well as the size of contracts. Some authorities have divided their work geographically (e.g. four contracts; north, south, east and west). Others have preferred a functional division (e.g. four contracts; groundsmanship, greenkeeping, tree work and ornamental horticulture). Again, the variety can help some contractors.

Some say (perhaps unfairly) that the division of work is so arranged to favour the local authority's own in-house bid. This may, or may not, be the case. An examination of the actual results of the contracts let tells a different story. As with every contract situation, there are always a number of surprises.

The need to expand

No in-house contractor may ever hope to be helped by the client more than external applicants. This is because the simple process of opening the tenders decides the winner. Only a contractor with a real will to win can hope to compete successfully.

All contractors know that complacency kills!

With contracts being let every year, there is great opportunity for all contractors who are keen to succeed. Some in-house contractors will succeed in being awarded contracts in adjacent authority areas. Some may lose their own authority's contract, yet succeed in those of a neighbouring authority.

The overriding requirement for every contractor is to be on his toes: 'be alert and active' is the motto of the successful landscape contractor.

The final area of growth for potential contractors is the park ranging and park keeping duties currently undertaken by local authorities. The government has included these duties in its leisure management competitive tendering regulations.

Many local authorities will include the outdoor leisure management arrangements within part of their grounds maintenance contract.

LEISURE MANAGEMENT

The outdoor leisure management aspects will include duties like taking football bookings, selling tennis tickets, and the ancillary tasks of opening changing-rooms and cleaning them afterwards. It is work with which the local authority based contractors will be all too familiar. However, it could mean a distinct change of operation for private contractors.

A seven-day-a-week operation will be necessary. Leisure, by its very nature, tends to mean unsocial working hours. Care and attention needs to be given to accurate costing, related to current wage rates in the area. It is very easy to make false assumptions about the availability and cost of suitable employees ready and able to undertake such duties.

The actual opening hours will be dictated by the client. So too will the prices to be charged. The authority will most likely decide annual increases, and inform the contractor accordingly. The contractor will charge the sports player that price (no more, no less). Depending on the specific clause within the contract, the contractor will either keep the income or return the income to the authority.

Most contracts will allow the contractor to retain the income; and require the contractor to provide detailed returns to the authority. This increased income to the contractor will allow for a slightly lower tender bid to be submitted in the first place. As with all estimating, it will be a matter for care and attention in deciding the likely annual income.

Income from fees and charges does bring with it a change to the usual fixed-price nature of a contract.

Income from sports facilities, by its very nature, is variable. Increased use can be stimulated by advertising, and promotional techniques. Many parks and recreation departments currently undertake a wide variety of promotions in their endeavour to increase use. In future it could be in the interests of the contractor to promote sports and games.

The more income that a park keeper can take means less cost to the contractor. The contractor has to pay the wages, whether the park keeper takes £1 or £100 per day. There will be many arguments and debates about this issue, in virtually every single contract.

Contractors will be well aware of marginal costing.

Leisure management will prove a real area of control, where this concept can be put into effect. Put simply, it is worth the contractor spending £1 where he can be assured he will receive more than £1 in return.

SUMMARY

This chapter has concentrated on possible areas of growth for contractors. Steady growth over a number of years is the usual occurrence for most successful businesses.

There is the opportunity for business extension, where a crisis has occurred in an adjacent contract. This has to be accurately managed. The key points of the chapter are as follows:

- All contractors start from small beginnings.
- Growth is assured by changing with the demands of the market-place.
- Growth can be achieved by slow expansion.
- Growth can also be achieved by being ready to help out when an adjacent contract runs into difficulties.
- Other contractors can appreciate assistance, as well as clients.
- Failed contracts always create difficult situations.
- In grounds maintenance failed contracts will be a new situation for many clients and contractors.
- Maintenance will totally cease (often after a protracted rundown).
- Members of the public, and sports players will soon voice their criticisms.
- Quick action is needed.
- Good communications are needed.

- Any contractor seeking new business needs to ensure a visible profile.
- It is not easy taking over after a failed contract – performance has to be exceptional despite the critical environment.
- Real skill at operating contracts needs to be developed, by every contractor.
- People skills are most important.
- Good supervisors are essential, as are key personnel with local knowledge.
- Most grounds maintenance contracts are considerably smaller than the other services subject to competitive tendering.
- The average contract is worth about £250 000, although there is considerable variation.
- At the beginning of the 1980s, four out of five contracts were being won by the public authority's own in-house contractor.
- Some 20% were won by independent contractors.
- Complacency is the biggest danger for any existing contractor.
- Leisure management (e.g. selling bowls tickets, taking football bookings) will often be added to grounds maintenance contracts.
- Where this occurs, there will often be an inbuilt incentive to the contractor to increase use and income.

No organization stays unchanged for long. It is either increasing in size or reducing. Most contractors are intent on expanding. They have to guard against the unexpected reduction which occurs from time to time.

Even local authority contractors have the opportunity to expand into other public maintenance contracts. The intention to grow, change and tackle new works is an essential ingredient for any contractor. That may well extend some landscape contractors, who become very keen games enthusiasts. If that increases general health and fitness, increases income to the contractor and reduces the cost to the client, then everyone will be winners.

ADDENDUM: RANGE OF EXPENDITURE ON PARKS

The extracts here are reproduced from the Audit Commission Occasional Paper, *Preparing for Compulsory Competition*; and from the Audit Commission publication, *Competitive Management of Parks and Green Spaces*. They are reproduced with the permission of the Controller of Her Majesty's Stationery Office.

Exhibit 4
Range of expenditure on parks

There is a wide range of expenditure within each type of local authority

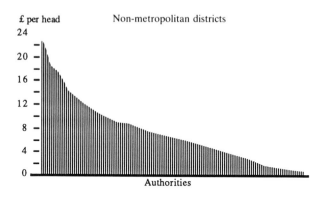

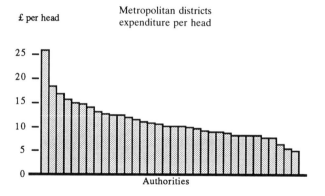

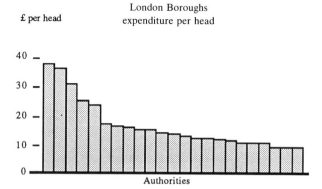

Note: These figures refer to all authorities in England and Wales
Source: CIPFA leisure and recreation estimates 1987–88

Exhibit 7

Maintenance standards for general amenity areas

The variations in standards are partly due to variations in climate, but other factors impinge

Authority	Specification		
	Cutting period	Frequency	Length mm
Bournemouth	March–Dec.	Every 14 days, 7 in peak	–
Babergh	April–Oct.	10 cuts	–
Bolton	April–Sept.	17 cuts	20–30
Lliw Valley	March–Oct.	Every 28 days, 14 in peak	30–60
Hillingdon	March–Nov.	12 cuts	25–75
South Bedfordshire	April–Sept.	Every 14 days	–
Windsor and Maidenhead	March–Nov.	14 cuts	25–75

Source: Audit Commission fieldwork

Exhibit 11

Range of tender prices for one ground maintenance contract

There can be substantial variation in the prices offered by different tenderers

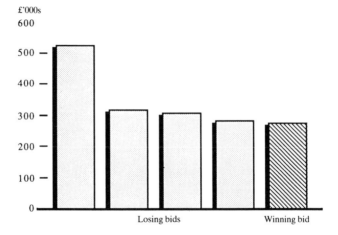

Source: Audit Commission fieldwork

Chapter Ten

Quality Assurance

There is a natural presumption in any contract that the quality and quantity of work undertaken will be constantly checked.

Every construction contract has a client clerk of works. Often this is a competent craftsman, who has made his way in life to being in charge of a contract, previously having been in charge of men. Often it is a very isolated position, one sandwiched between the client and the contractor.

THE CLERK OF WORKS

Every authority committed to maintaning standards will have a strong contingent of Inspectors, Supervisors/Clerks of Work. The titles will be numerous, but their work is the same. Their duties will be to programme work, order it from the contractor, check that it is done exactly as stated in the specification, then pay up.

It is all reminiscent of the old foreman. The one who would stand over a gang of men all day, and ensure that they worked hard and strong. Apart from getting cold, he did nothing. Or, at least, that was the theory.

Similar principles will apply to contracts. The Clerk of Works, of course, will not physically stand over each gang; those days, at least, have long since gone. Furthermore, he will be in charge of many different teams all around the district.

SUPERVISION AND CONTROL

The Audit Commision state that one inspector should be able to supervise over £500 000 worth of works. Well, that remains to be seen, but there can be no doubt that each Clerk of Works will have a multiplicity of tasks over a wide area.

The only way to manage a wide diversity of tasks is by close control.

The Clerk of Works will require the contractor to attend weekly meetings. These will be to map out the work for the week ahead, and also to check on any difficulties from the previous week. Finally, he will arrange for payment.

This is always a good time for a contractor to press for prompt payment.

PAYMENTS

The tender document (as with everything else) will give details of when payment becomes due to the contractor. Contractors need to enforce it. Furthermore, it pays to check what are the penalties if the client fails to pay within a given time period. For the contractor, it is not just standards that matter, but also early payment. Prompt payment is another ingredient which leads to profit.

DAILY MEETINGS

In most contracts there will also be daily meetings with the on-site supervisors. The Clerk of Works could be in charge of the work of six or more teams, with up to five or six men in each team; these teams will be spread over a district of many square miles. He needs to know where they are, otherwise he will spend many a fruitless hour playing hide-and-seek with the contractor's workforce. He will be unable to check on the standards of work undertaken if he knows not where or when the work is being carried out.

So daily meetings will be necessary. Once a routine has been established, these daily meetings should benefit both contractor and client.

VARIATION ORDERS AND PRICING

One way in which it will benefit the contractor is the multitude of variation orders and one-off jobs required. The weather will also determine some priorities. So will local demands.

Local authorities know that a sure way of satisfying an upset resident is to go and get the complaint sorted out and rectified. Residents do not take too kindly to being told that their complaint will be seen to the next time the team calls by and this could be some six weeks away. The letters column in the local newspaper, at least appears weekly.

This is also true of one-off works required in a playground or playing field or a cemetery or in a multitude of different situations. Immediate attention is needed.

In a few cases, even waiting a day will be too long: if a security fence has been breached the night before, closing the gap cannot wait another night. That would be tantamount to issuing an invitation to the criminals to come back and break in again. Action the same day is essential.

Provided the prices quoted by the contractor are agreeable to the client, a flow of many individual, one-off jobs is guaranteed. A welcome change to any contractor. It will allow him to break out of the priced straitjacket imposed by the costed tender. Given that the contractor ensures constant attention to the price, a stream of variation orders will come his way.

The price is crucial. A shopkeeper makes little or no profit on basic commodities such as bread and milk, whereas the highest profit comes from luxury and impulse purchases. It is the same with grounds maintenance. Apart from the all-important price, the other crucial aspect both to client and contractor is quality.

The Clerk of Works will be especially keen to ensure that the quality of works undertaken is to the highest possible standard. Not only is that his job, he also has many people behind him, demanding that he gets the highest standard.

Fig. 10.1   Urgent tasks pay well

COMPLAINTS AND PENALTIES

No matter how competently fine turf is maintained, there will be complaints. Complaints tend to increase when the home team loses. Cricket teams are especially notorious for blaming the state of the pitch.

Where the maintenance is actually at fault, the Clerk of Works will be called to an inquiry. In his turn, he will have to ensure better maintenance in future from the contractor. He will impose the required improvements on the contractor by a number of different means – from verbal requests to written warnings, and/or deductions from payments due. If warnings are not heeded and poor workmanship continues, then ultimately a contract will be terminated. A terminated contract means failure for both parties.

SATISFACTION

Similarly, with the individual, one-off jobs passed to the contractor, good workmanship is essential. Profit is essential too, but it is also of paramount importance to ensure that the customer is satisfied. In this case, the customer is the local resident who complained or requested attention to some special task or asked for a tree to be trimmed to allow more light into the house.

If the customer is not satisfied, then the contractor will not be satisfied. The Clerk of Works will see to that. Therefore, to ensure that adequate standards are achieved, a contractor will need to appoint his own supervisors.

Indeed these supervisors will often be the key to a successful contract. Too often, contracts have gone sour for want of adequate supervision by the contractor. Indoctrinating profitable practices in each team leader is one side of the coin, ensuring that standards are achieved is the other. This leads to the somewhat ludicrous, yet common, situation whereby the client employs a Clerk of Works to supervise a supervisor appointed by the contractor.

WHO SUPERVISES THE SUPERVISORS?

The contractors supervisor, in turn, supervises the contract teams. Daft or not, this is a simple fact of life for many contracts. It has to be: without adequate communication, standards will fall. Tasks will not be carried out. Complaints will follow from residents and sports players which, in turn, will lead to pressure being exerted on the contractor.

But surely there is at least one supervisor too many? Indeed it could be argued that if the contractor could be trusted to do the job correctly in the first place, there are two supervisors too many. There is no easy answer to this one.

On the one hand, there is the commonsense belief that one supervisor should be sufficient. On the other hand, experience has shown (and bitter experience as well, for that matter) that one supervisor is needed by the client and one supervisor is needed by the contractor.

However, increased supervisory costs is an accepted feature of competitive tendering in managing maintenance services by contract. The government openly acknowledge that costs of management will increase.

These increased costs, the government argues, will be more than offset by the savings in the actual maintenance operations themselves. These savings will be brought about by the very nature of competition in the free-market place.

So be it; but many will see the increased supervision required as being a direct result of the need to supervise closely landscape contractors of unknown pedigree.

This, of course, goes to the very heart of the agony of many competent professional landscape contractors: they see 'cowboy' contractors cutting corners.

Oddly, this is one area where both public and private sector contractors agree. Both see their years of experience and professionalism being thrown to the winds. Neither can compete with 'here today, gone tomorrow' landscape contractors.

It has to be said that this aspect has been foreseen. The need to employ competent contractors has led directly to the many controls and checks being made at the tendering stage.

The very nature of this high-profile public service will demand that the highest standards of care are seen to be provided. This will be possible, given strict supervision by both client and contractor.

Fig. 10.2 Two supervisors instead of one will naturally double the costs involved

There appears to be only one way of reducing the duplication of supervisory effort. This is by means of entrusting the contractor with supervising his own work. At the 1990s progress, increased onus will be placed on contractors adequately to supervise their own works.

BRITISH STANDARDS

In manufacturing industry a whole method of in-house supervision has been implemented through Quality Assurance. Here an important British Standard places on the contractor a real degree of trust. Not only trust in controlling the quality of the workmanship, but also in the contractor's technical ability to provide that standard in the first place.

This is good news for competent contractors.

The first batch of contracts made little reference to the British Standard, or even to Quality Assurance itself.

QUALITY ASSURANCE

However, since many grounds maintenance contracts will be let out to tender each year, there is plenty of opportunity for the client to include reference to BS 5750 in his future contracts. Quality Assurance guidelines suitable for grounds maintenance, and the other local authority services subject to maintenance contracting, will be increasingly evident as the years go by.

As with manufacturing industry, it makes sense, and more important, reduces costs for work to be Quality Assured by the contractor. The assurance given by the contractor radically alters the burden of inspection and supervision, for Quality Assurance is more powerful than simple quality control.

That does not mean to say that supervisors will not be needed. They will, both on the contract side and the client side; but there should be needed many fewer, especially on the client side. It should be possible for a lesser percentage of the work to be checked where trust and confidence have been formally established with the contractor.

That raises the issues as to what penalty would be appropriate if faults are identified. Say a Clerk of Works only inspects 10% of the work of a Quality Assured contractor. On an inspection one day, he finds that two flower beds are not weeded, as they should have been, while the other eight are satisfactory. The Clerk of Works also knows that there are 100 flower beds altogether in the district. Should he delay payment on only the two flower beds, until they have been reworked, or more? Another example could relate to an unmarked cricket pitch.

Immeasurable defaults

Nothing would compensate the cricket team for not having the pitch marked out and ready for play on the day of their revenge match against their local opponents. No matter how thoroughly the pitch had been prepared during the week, no matter how clean the pavilion, the simple mistake of not marking out the pitch and field for the first game of the season would mean the total disatisfaction of the cricket team.

Would it be warranted to withhold all payments due to the contractor for the preparation of the pitch? Or just the payment due for the marking of the pitch?

That is a difficult one.

Gamesmanship

A similar situation could easily occur at the golf course. If new holes are cut in the middle of a two-day tournament, the tournament would have to be totally abandoned.

Going back to the flower bed example, it would mean withholding payment on 20 beds. Yet only two beds were seen to be unweeded. To withhold payment on 20 beds, in these circumstances, would be fiercely contested by any contractor. Withholding payments on unsubstantiated claims could not be tolerated.

Trust

But then, that is precisely where trust and confidence comes in. If the absurdity of double doses of supervision is to be avoided, then confidence in the contractor supervising his own work has to be established. That may mean it being established the hard way. Hopefully, professional landscape contractors will have no qualms about entering into such a Quality Assurance agreement. The 'cowboys' can and should be beaten.

Close supervision for both client and contractor needs to be the order of the day in most contracts – from the beginning. This should give way to a more trusting and confident relationship as the contract progresses. This will immeasurably help the contractor. No contractor can afford withheld payments. No contractor can afford the lost time spent rectifying mistakes.

Quality-assured

It is likely that certification for Quality Assurance will be forthcoming only after the contract has been operational for a couple of years. But that is the detail which will be covered in the tender document and the relevant British Standard.

There is real benefit in a contractor being Quality Assured. Not only will supervision costs be reduced, but also there will be less delayed payments (while an area is reworked). Furthermore, in future years there will be an increased demand for contractors who carry the Quality Assured label.

SUMMARY

Further details of Quality Assurance are given in the Addendum to this chapter. Before looking into the details, the key issues discussed in this chapter relating to quality control for contractors need to be highlighted:

- Most contracts will be tightly supervised.
- Local residents and sports players will demand high standards.
- A client Clerk of Works will regularly (daily and weekly) liaise with the contractor's managers and supervisors.
- Regular effective liaison will provide for a smooth contract (high standards for the client; and prompt payments for the contractor).
- Grounds maintenance is a high-profile public service – get it wrong and everyone shouts.
- Effective procedures are needed by the contractor to ensure complaints are quickly and adequately dealt with.
- Quality control will become of paramount importance.
- This emphasis on high standards leads to an unnecessary level of supervision.
- Both client and contractor will need supervisors checking the same work.
- If the contractor can be trusted, the level of client supervision can be reduced.
- This can also mean penalties increasing where faults are found.
- Increasingly, contracts will include reference to BS 5750, Quality Assurance.
- This provides an agreed method of quality systems and passes increased responsibility to the contractor.
- To be Quality Assured should be the aim of all professional contractors.

- The requirement to become Quality Assured (within a year or two of contract start) will be increasingly incorporated into tenders.
- Quality Assurance should not be confused with Quality Control, which is more limited.
- Quality Assurance is a powerful tool and radically alters the relationship between client and contractor – to both contractor's and client's benefit.
- Quality Assurance is most importantly of benefit to the contract.

Quality Assurance is a concept originally introduced in industry. It is a powerful tool to ensure that a uniform quality product is produced every time. Furthermore, the Quality Assurance scheme leaves the responsibility for supervision where it belongs – namely, with the contractor producing the goods or services. Formal annual review ensures the quality system is maintained.

Some form of quality assessment is essential in grounds maintenance, for the sake both of client and contractor. The introduction of a Quality Assurance code offers both parties to a contract the best form of standard assessment. More important for the contractor is that the label Quality Assured will be the biggest bonus he could wish to achieve.

ADDENDUM: QUALITY ASSURANCE GUIDELINES

Reproduced here is the basis for a Quality Assurance scheme. It is provided by kind permission of the Institute of Quality Assurance, from their publication, *Quality Assurance, Cleansing Services, Grounds Maintenance and Leisure Facilities*, 1990.

Objectives
The purpose of this document is to outline how Quality Assessment under BS 5750:1987 can be implemented for the services covered by the Local Government Act 1988; whether they be undertaken by contractors or DSOs. In essence, BS 5750 is a codification of sound managerial practice. It specifies the organisational criteria that must be met by a supplier's system of management to assure consistent quality. These criteria were developed mainly in manufacturing industry, but they comprise organisational practices common to services and production alike, and have been adopted world-wide through the ISO 9000 series of specifications.

So far attention has been given to refuse collection, other cleaning, the cleaning of buildings, grounds maintenance, and very recently, leisure facilities. Each of these services is covered in a separate Appendix, and it is expected that further Appendices covering catering, vehicle maintenance and highways and construction will be added in due course. The application of QA to education and other local authority areas, social services for example, is also under review.

Although, at the time of writing, there is very little practical experience available of quality assessment in respect of local government services this document does synthesise the collective experience of those who are familiar with QA and the services in question. In this respect the prime purpose of this document is to publish what is known in order to assist those seeking quality assessment in local government, and to help those in QA who may be unfamiliar with local authority services.

The ultimate objective of these guidance notes is to assist in the improvement of the quality of services provided by local government. To this end we must not forget the real customer; the public who use the services local authorities provide. It is their needs that must be paramount, not those of the supplier, or the client organisation for that matter. Today's QA philosophy is customer-centred, it embraces marketing and gives primacy to the ultimate customer. This Total Quality Management approach is not simply a question of techniques, but a reflection of an organisation's underlying commitment to those it serves.

Client and contractor relations.
In specifying that contractors must seek to be quality assessed and certified in accordance with BS 5750:1987, authorities are making a commitment to quality that must be reflected at all levels. Quality is quite sensitive to good client/contractor relations, if they are bad quality will suffer. Nor is QA a remedy for poor management, the remedies for that must lie elsewhere. We should see BS 5750 as a basic code of good practice, simply the starting point for sound management. If people cannot meet this minimal criteria then something is seriously wrong.

In order to specify that a contractor seeks certification a contract clause is required to the effect that, "The contractor must obtain certification for the specified services in accordance with BS 5750:1987 through a Certifying Body approved by the NACCB within a specified period, and to retain certification thereafter." A minimum of 12 months from the commencement of a contract is felt to be reasonable in most cases. Prior certification is not possible because certification can only apply to existing services and not paper proposals.

The Local Government Act 1988 does not preclude questions regarding a tenderer's proposed management system, and client authorities should give firm guidance on the timetable required for gaining certification. Alternatively, the client could require prospective contractors to submit their own certification timetable, and take account of this when awarding the contract. It is not suggested that a failure to gain certification should, of itself, warrant contract termination. However, if the contractor lacks the commitment to introduce an adequate quality system it is most likely that the quality of service would be such so as to warrant termination in any event.

A contractor certified for a particular service in one local authority would, other things being equal, need only reproduce the same quality management system for a new authority to obtain another certificate. Government grants are available to help smaller firms obtain the consultancy help needed to get started with certification. Where the service is in-house the requirements for certification will be identical to those applied to a contractor. In any case, contractors and DSOs would be wise to have a quality system in accordance with BS 5750 as a matter of good practice even where this is not a contract requirement.

Any service that is Quality Assessed and duly certified will be subject to surveillance at least twice a year by the Certification Body that awarded the certificate. Nevertheless it is still the responsibility of the certificate holder to ensure that his system is being maintained, and to this end he should carry out his own programme of internal audits to ensure that his system is being implemented, and is efficient and effective.

Standards and monitoring.
A clear concise contract is vital to success in contracting-out. Work must clearly be specified, and there must be no room for dispute as to what the contractor is asked to do. The contractor can only be judged on what is in the contract. If he has been told to sweep a street once a week it is not his fault if, having done so properly, the street is dirty two days later. In such a case the specification was wrong, not the contractor. But how clean is clean? Attempts have been made to measure the cleanliness of floors; to photograph streets and count the items of litter, etc, but as yet no techniques are available that can be incorporated in a legal contract. Clients are thus reliant on visual inspection and the experienced eye to determine whether the work has been done to an agreed visual standard.

Fortunately BS 5701:1980 on Number Defective Control Charts
provides a sound sampling scheme for processes where only visual
inspection is possible – whether a job has been done correctly or
not. Experience to date suggests that it is quite possible to
evolve consistent levels of visual consensus between council
officers and the contractor's supervisory staff as to what constitutes an adequate standard. Quality certification requires
that three factors, amongst others, be demonstrated. Firstly,
that the quality level has been specified. Secondly, that the
specified quality is then properly monitored and measured.
Thirdly, that the people who do this monitoring and measuring are
competent to so do.

To satisfy these requirements the factors that constitute the
required standard must be written into the contract. The characteristics of a clean street, for example, should be included in
the contract specification – clean gulleys, litter removed from
footways, etc. It is then a matter of inspecting the work to an
agreed visual standard on a day to day basis. Inspectors skilled
in judging whether the standard has been reached are essential –
working to either a 100% inspection system (The control of fly-
tipping, vandalism, etc, might demand this) or a random sampling
inspection regime based on BS 5701 or the BS 6000 series.

What is BS 5750:1987?
This British Standard forms the basis for civilian consumer-
orientated quality systems in Britain, and it is identical to the
ISO 9000 series of standards used throughout the world. It has
three parts. Part One is for organisations where there is a
significant design responsibility. Part Two of BS 5750 covers
organisations that produce either goods or services to
established specifications, and it is this part that is relevant
to the services under discussion. Part Three covers systems for
final inspections and tests.

It is worth stressing yet again that BS 5750 is best seen as the
codification of sound management practice. It provides a framework of good practice that ensures consistent levels of product
or service to the specified quality. It is for the client to
specify the service quality: adherence to BS 5750 simply means
that the client's specifications will be consistently met. It is
for this reason that many sectors of the economy will only accept
tenders from 'quality assessed' organisations. Whilst this does
not remove a client's right to determine standards, it does in
fact reduce the required amount inspection and supervision.

The Appendices that follow on from here should be read with Part
Two of BS 5750. The full title is:- "BS 5750: Part 2:1987.
Quality systems. Part 2. Specification for production and
installation." The term, "production and installation," should
simply be read as, "supply of service." Likewise, where the
term, "product," is used, "service" should be substituted. It is
a fact of life that almost all of the management techniques used
in local government have industrial origins and the language of

British Standards in the field of Quality reflects this, but this
in no way detracts from their usefulness in the service sector.

It is worth noting that the supporting document in the British
Standard, "Guide to quality management and quality system
elements. BS 5750: Part 0: Section 0.2: 1987 (ISO 9004: 1987),"
does include services throughout its terminology. In its introduction, for example, it says that, "In order to be successful, a
company must offer products or services that...." In due course
it is hoped that all of BS 5750/ISO 9000 will be using the
language of the services sector, and indeed the BQA has already
taken some initiatives in this direction.

The interpretations of BS 5750:1987 that follows is based on the
Sector Committee's assessment of how the British Standard relates
to refuse collection, building cleaning, other cleaning, ground
maintenance and leisure services. Many of the requirements are
self-explanatory, but some are not and these notes are intended
to help consultants, contractors, clients and Certifying Bodies
alike. In order to follow these interpretations it is advised
that they be read with a copy of BS 5750, Part 2, at hand.

Activities where security is important.
These guidance notes are primarily addressed to the needs of
local authorities operating in the ordinary course of their
everyday duties. Nevertheless, Central Government, Military,
Civil Aviation, and similar such authorities will find these
notes of equal value when employing contractors for the services
to which these notes relate. Further, they may also find that
any special requirements with respect to security – contractor's
employee vetting procedures, the monitoring of a contractor's
security arrangements, etc – would be met more readily within the
disciplined framework of an audited quality management system.

APPENDIX 4: interpreting BS 5750 for grounds maintenance.

The Standard is in various parts thus:-

1   Scope and field of application.
This clause starts with, "This International Standard specifies
the quality system requirements for use where a contract between
two parties requires demonstration of a supplier's capability to
control processes that determine the acceptability of product
supplied." The requirements specified in this Standard are aimed
primarily at preventing and detecting any nonconformity in
performing the services, and implementing the means to prevent
the occurrence of nonconformities. It goes on to say that it,
"is applicable in contractual situations when

   a) the specified requirements for product are stated in
   terms of an established design or specification;

   b) confidence in product conformance can be attained by
   adequate demonstration of a certain supplier's capabilities
   in production and installation."

The Standard uses the word, "product," and the term, "production
and installation." By substituting the word, "service," and the
term, "operation and application," respectively the language
becomes appropriate for grounds maintenance services. Clauses 2
and 3 of the Standard refer to references and definitions and
need not be examined here. Thus:-

4   Quality system requirements
This clause is the main clause in the Standard. It is divided
into many sub-clauses and each outlines a specific requirement on
the contractor's part. Thus:-

4.1 Management responsibility
Quality policy should be understood at all levels of the organisation. The documentation will include a quality manual -
defining policy and objectives for, and commitment to, quality -
with quality plans appropriate to the service, site and contract.
The responsibilities of the supplier's head office and site staff
should be clearly defined in the manual: identifying the in-built
inspection system and standards employed, along with a method of
system audit using staff not directly responsible for the work.
A management representative must be available, responsible for
monitoring the implementation and upkeep of the quality system.

4.2 Quality system
This requires that the contractor should have a properly
documented quality system. The notes in this sub-clause refer to
the definition of quality objectives, allocation of responsibilities, written procedures, inspection and audit programmes.
Items (b), (d) and (f) are thought not to apply, but the rest do.

4.3 Contract review
The client and contractor must understand and agree the scope and
conditions of the contract prior to commencing the service. They
must regularly review the working contract, to agree improvements
and modifications in the light of experience, and to agree any
work variations: additional flower beds, higher standards, etc.

4.4 Document control
The key to good housekeeping. Records of scheduled work, or
missed grass cutting, the condition of mechanical plant, the tree
programme, etc, must be under control; updatings recorded, and
they must be someone's particular responsibility. When records,
work instructions, etc, are superseded, this should be clearly
indicated so as not to mislead through outdated information. A
system to prove the issue of documents is a requirement. This
requirement applies in particular to the Quality Manual, the
Quality Plan, and to all related quality records.

4.5 Purchasing
This part relates to the purchase, by the contractor, of trees,
shrubs, mowers, vehicle servicing, training services, tools, and
so on. The specification of purchased items must be suitable for
their purpose, a system of inspection employed, and adequate
documentation used to monitor their service life and performance.

4.6 Purchaser supplied product
Where the local authority supplies the contractor with certain
items; bulbs, saplings, for example, the contractor must ensure
that the materials supplied are fit for their purpose, to store
them in a suitable manner, and maintain records to monitor their
quality standard.

4.7 Product identification and traceability
For, "product," substitute, "service." This requirement applies,
as it stands. Who weeded that plot, or was in charge of the
grave digging? Activities must be recorded so that the service
can be identified and traced.

4.8 Process control
This covers the basic planning required by any grounds maintenance service, essentially this clause requires that the operational control be thought through and documented - the summer and
winter work schedules, staff needed and reporting procedures.
However, 4.8.2 (Special processes) needs attention if the sevice
includes processes where the effects would not be noticed for
some time. This would apply if chemicals are used; weed-killers,
growth retardants, fertilizers, etc. The key here is to concentrate on getting the method right, ie, staff trained in the implementation of the procedure, and adequate call-back facilities.

4.9 Inspection and testing
Generally the service will be 'final inspection' only with visual
standards agreed between the local authority and the supplier.
Records of the inspections carried out each day must be kept.

4.10 Inspection, measuring and test equipment.
This clause is not thought to apply to grounds maintenance.

4.11 Inspection and test status
Not applicable. The status of inspection of any area of work is by reference to the inspection records.

4.12 Control of nonconforming product
This applies to calling back for missed pruning, or re-weeding a badly weeded grave, etc. The procedures required here relate to service failure: ensuring that such failures are properly recorded and are acted upon without delay.

4.13 Corrective action
This covers need to have procedures for determining the cause of sub-standard or non-conforming work, complaints, etc, and the need to take appropriate action to prevent its re-occurance.

4.14 Handling, storage, packaging and delivery
Procedures for handling, storage delivery and disposal of chemicals, shrubs, saplings, etc, in the execution of the service shall acccord with the contract's requirements and statutory regulations and bye laws.

4.15 Quality records
This part of the Standard identifies the factors that should be reflected in sound quality record practice. It includes the results of random surveys, the keeping of control charts, etc.

4.16 Internal quality audits
The service supplier must audit the effectiveness of the quality system in accordance with a written procedure and schedule, using someone without direct responsibility for the service. On large sites this could be done by a member of the site's management team, but on smaller sites with fewer personnel a representative from head office or from another site might be more appropriate.

4.17 Training
This relates to people being trained in the procedures documented by the contractor, which will include safe working methods. Staff must be trained to do the job in hand, and the work must be adequately documented so as to permit new staff to understand procedures. (NB. It has been suggested that this might conflict with the 'non-commercial' clauses of the Local Government Act 1988. It is thought not to, but in any event it is the Certification Body that will make any inquiries in this context).

4.18 Statistical techniques
This covers the methods used for inspection and work sampling. BS 5701:1980 and the BS 6000 series would cover the services in this Appendix, but that does not exclude other sampling plans.

Chapter Eleven

In time, in touch, in profit

The final, all-important task to achieve is, of course, running the contract successfully and profitably for the full three to six years of its duration.

OPERATIONAL, TO LAST THREE TO SIX YEARS

Having overcome all the hurdles on the way to success, a contractor could be forgiven for relaxing. After all, a contractor who has been successful in the unknown territory of tender documents, tight timescales, and the like, is bound to succeed on his home territory of grounds maintenance. An easy trap may be waiting here for the contractor to fall into. Case-studies have indicated that even the most well-known companies have been known to fail.

Indeed, any contractor who relaxes, at any time, will soon find himself in trouble. One person, in particular, will be far from forgiving – namely the client. The client will pursue the contractor to the end; and this will be long after the contractor has ceased working for the authority. It will be undertaken by the independent arbitrators, or if that fails, a court of law. The fearful fact is that all authorities are highly competent and experienced in dealing with failed contractors. A contractor cannot hope to equal the resources of time and cash which an authority can muster.

The winning of the tender is undoubtedly the last hurdle to overcome in that particular race.

Yet another race starts immediately; but this one is more of a marathon. And the tactics and skills employed for the first race are useless for the second.

Pacing

The enduring marathon running needs to establish a regular stride, relaxed breathing and a running stride to suit his body build. The runner needs to keep going. He also needs to beware of sudden interruption, the odd crisis, for it could be disastrous. A stray dog barking at the heels of the runner can so destroy his rhythm that he collapses minutes later in exhaustion. Taking a wrong turn on a poorly marshalled event can be equally devastating.

The sudden surge in panic, excitement and emotion is difficult to control. It takes an experienced runner to be able to regain his basic rhythm and, moreover, regain it sufficiently quickly.

Success in business is just the same: a systematic routine is essential.

Appropriate methods in horticulture

The strength of the routine depends upon close applicability to the nature of the business. A number of key factors for a successful business have been examined in this book.

Examples would include those seaside landladies who work flat-out during the British holiday season, then holiday on the Mediterranean for a month or two in the winter. Or look at the routine of a corner shopkeeper, maintaining meticulous records year on year, for comparison. Even large retailing businesses keep an exact check on receipts every single day.

The secret of ongoing success is to find (and use) the correct combination of basic monitoring systems. Each business, each contract, differs; but there are a number of basic monitoring tools which we have already examined:

- The client demands works to be undertaken at exactly the right time.
- The contractor needs to keep constantly in touch with the client, as well as with his own workforces, wherever they may be.
- Each individual task needs to be carried out at a profit.
- Horticulture is successful only by individual teamwork.
- Grounds maintenance on a dozen sites spread over miles is very different to factory-floor management.
- Individual working is one of the greatest strengths (and sources of satisfaction) to those in amenity horticulture.
- It is also a great weakness.
- Few have direct experience of working to a detailed written specification.

Somehow all these weaknesses and strengths have to be brought together for the overall benefit of the contract. They have to come together in a coherent manner, which is in total accord with the actual contract being operated. There is no better place to start than with the Specification.

THE PRICED SPECIFICATION

The Specification states exactly how each individual task is to be carried out. More important, the contractor has given his price for carrying out each of these tasks. He has arrived at that price by taking into account all the on-costs, the time lost in travelling, etc. He has also incorporated his best-known methods of undertaking the work. He will win only by keeping to those prices – or a little less. The next step is to translate this priced Specification into a comprehensive costing system.

This is harder than it sounds. It is far too easy to just reproduce the Specification in all its glorious detail. This leads to masses of paper for each and every task, and the sheer quantity means that the information contained is rendered useless. This is because, quite simply, no one has the time to read it. And worse still, sometimes the busy groundsman cannot understand it.

Computer companies have all had to grapple with this basic problem. Many of the computer systems on offer have much to commend them. However, it is worthwhile subjecting any system – computer or otherwise – to a simple test.

Does the monitoring system relate the tendered price to the actual work undertaken in a simple manner? A typical item in a Specification would be as shown in Table 11.1.

For a meaningful order to be issued to a works team, the quantity and the site need to be added.

A WORKS SCHEDULE

Quantities and sites are often stated separately (in the Bills of Quantities section for example). Either the client or the contractor will need to bring

Table 11.1   A detailed specification

Item no.	Specification	Unit	Price (£)
A123	Hedge cutting. Cut cleanly all hedges with approved equipment to a height of 5 ft and width 4 ft, with straight top and sides. Rake out all debris from under the hedge and dispose of it at the approved tip, together with all arisings from the work. Leave site clean and tidy at the end of each working day.	lin. m	3.00

together an order of working for each team. The exact responsibility will either be stated in the tender document or be left to the contractor.

It is in the interests of both parties, however, to have an agreed programme of works. Therefore the client should assist, at least in part, in the bringing together of a composite work programme.

The first stage would be to prepare a simplified schedule of works, which is closely related to the Specification and Bill of Quantities. An adequate system will need to provide the necessary information to both client and contractor. Both are interested in the quality and the correct timing of the work. A simple system is called for, which does not entail reams of paper. The example for hedge cutting, given above, could be changed to that in Table 11.2.

Table 11.2 An abbreviated specification

Item no.	Description	Site	Quantity/ frequency	Unit	Price (£)	Hours
A123	Hedge cut	KGV p.f.	500	lin. m	1 500	80

The key elements of the Specification are repeated in this brief job order or work schedule:

Item no.	This refers the job order back to the Specification. It will be an integral part of the tender document to cut the hedge entirely as stated in the Specification and not as stated in the abbreviated job order or work schedule.
Description	The minimum amount of description here, to identify the task.
Site	All sites will be specified in the tender documents and accompanying maps. This site refers to the King George V playing-field.
Quantity/ frequency	The quantity or frequency will give the amount of work to be undertaken. For hedge cutting, only the total linear metres are given (e.g. 500). For a bowling-green, it would be more appropriate to state the frequency (e.g. swish 7 times per week).
Unit	The unit of measurement is transferred directly from the Specification.
Price	The price is that tendered by the contractor who tendered £3 per linear metre. Thus the price will be £1 500 for 500 linear metres.

Hours   The crucial information to the contractor is the target hours. This determines his profit or loss.

The tabular information, given above, will start to give some meaningful facts and figures to the contractor in managing the contract. To be successful in so doing, the contractor needs to be able constantly to monitor profit-and-loss situation.

Scheduled profit

Profitability is based entirely upon keeping to the tendered price. This, in turn, means keeping to the hours actually targeted for the job. The hours of work which the contractor thought each task would take need to be closely monitored. A schedule of work is also essential to the client for his adequate monitoring.

Taking the example in Table 11.2, it is relatively easy to build up a weekly, monthly or even yearly schedule. Say one week's work for a team was at the town's King George V playing-field and the adjacent Beech Meadows housing area. A week's work ticket would resemble that shown in Table 11.3.

This particular table provides an excellent guide both for the client and the contractor. Each needs to know what work is being undertaken during any particular week, and the value of that work. However, only contractors need to know the actual hours; the last column should not be shown to the client.

Table 11.3   A specification based work programme

Item no.	Description	Site	Quantity/ frequency	Unit	Price (£)	Hours
A123	Hedge cut	KGV	500	lin. m	1 500	80
B456	Bowling-green cut	KGV	× 3	/green	100	5
C678	Pavilion clean	KGV	× 7	/pav.	120	7
D987	Litter	KGV	× 7	/p. f.	120	7
E654	Triple mow	KGV	× 1	/p. f.	60	2
D987	Litter	BMH	12 000	m²	70	4
E654	Triple mow	BMH	30 000	m²	150	5
G234	Strim	BMH	1 000	lin. m	100	35
F321	Beds, cultivate	BMH	2 000	m²	1 200	70
			Totals		3 420	1 854

Note: Figures are illustrative only.

These principles have been taken by computer companies as the basis for their computer applications. However, there is a danger in buying computer software off the peg because it is not designed for a specific contract. Equally important, most users abdicate all responsibility when they sign the order to the computer company.

MIY or DIY?

An example is given in the Addendum to this chpater, where a Manage-it-Yourself approach has been taken. Such systems allow practising landscape contractors to build up their own systems in the manner of their own choosing. There is no reason why it cannot be linked to a client ordering system as well.

The Manage-it-Yourself approach has a lot of offer. It concentrates the mind. The computer becomes but a facilitator to the end-product, at no time does it take over. The manager is always left to manage.

Homespun systems often turn out to be the best, for they have been tailor-made for a given situation.

In horticultural contracts there are many variable factors such as the soil and climate. Weather conditions vary from year to year and, of course, the staff employed change. All horticulturists vary, horticulture allows the individual preferences of working methods to be retained.

So the ongoing paper monitoring systems must be able to take account of all those variables. A good farm secretary would be quite at home compiling a suitable system. It does not take specific accountancy training to be able to formulate such a system. The details in this chapter (and Addendum) give examples of how to build up individual systems for contracts.

Computers and office records

The widespread use of computers is not due to any major difficulty contained in the information that is to be recorded. The principal purpose of those computer systems in general use is to deal readily with the quantity of information involved. The office administrator is more likely to be daunted by the actual quantity of records rather than its difficulty.

Whatever the system used (manual or computer, bought in or home produced), its success will depend on its appropriateness to the circumstances. The key features which a successful system needs to include are the following:

1. date by which maintenance work must commence;
2. latest date by which work is to be completely finished;

3. exact description of work (or more likely, a number referring to an exact description);
4. site;
5. frequency;
6. tendered price;
7. estimated manhours for the work to be undertaken;
8. actual hours taken;
9. actual cost;
10. actual profit or loss.

The importance of this essential record cannot be overstated for a continuingly successful operation. All the key features listed above, then need to be bound together into one work scheduling form. Thus the contractor is in a position to adequately monitor each and every working team. More important, each team can monitor its own performance. Profit and loss have to be assessed, at least once, every single week.

THE CLIENT

The client will also need a schedule of work, so that his Clerk of Works can adequately monitor progress. This timetable or programme can, of course, be prepared by the client; but it is for the client to decide which party will prepare this schedule.

There are benefits in the contractor detailing the schedule. He can then so organize his work as to undertake the maximum workload in the minimum time.

Some clients might not require a schedule at all. They will rely on the frequencies stated in the contract documentation. The work has then to be undertaken exactly as stated in these documents.

However, due to the complexity and quantity of different grounds maintenance operations, it will take many years of contract operations before the client acquires sufficient confidence to rely on only the contract document.

PAYROLL/PRODUCTIVITY

The flow of weekly or monthly forms will determine the continuing success of a contract. Further additions could be made to the form to include the weekly hours worked by each member of the team. This can be linked with the relevent details for payroll, although such a system may prove to be too complex. Payroll details and work scheduling are perhaps best kept separately. However, there must be the closest link between the two.

SUMMARY

It needs careful, detailed thought and preparation to transfer the elation of winning a contract into a day-by-day, week-by-week and year-by-year successful grounds maintenance operation. Key features include the following:

- The successful contractor must never relax.
- Running the contract will be even harder than submitting the tender.
- But running the contract will be home territory for most.
- The client will pay critical attention to performance.
- Public authorities are well-versed in enforcing contracts.
- A contractor must therefore ensure that the Conditions of Contract are never seriously used against him.
- The success of a marathon runner lies in his ability to set a sustainable pace.
- Once set, he must endeavour to keep to that pace.
- His success depends entirely on his rhythm.
- Grounds maintenance operations are the same.
- A given weekly (and seasonal) pace will be essential to success.
- The successful contractor intermixes all the key features of his contract onto a monitoring form.
- The real key to success is to keep it simple.
- Most tasks, no matter how big, should be reduced to one line on a work programming form.
- A purchased paperwork system (manual or computerized) should not be imposed by an outside company, rather it should be built up by the contractor.
- There should be a weekly assessment of profit and loss.

The key to continuing success in a contract is continuous close monitoring. Paperwork systems must be based on the tender, and the tendered price. All monitoring will then relate exactly to the client's Specification, and also to the contractor's bid price. There can be no sounder method of establishing continued confidence and success.

ADDENDUM: GROUNDS MAINTENANCE CONTRACT

Profit or loss calculations

The simple systems noted below lend themselves to many grounds maintenance situations. The calculations can be undertaken manually, or with a pocket calculator. The systems also lend themselves to a small computer/spreadsheet application. Constant control is achieved by entry of the actual hours taken for each task.

ANALYSIS OF REGULAR/CYCLICAL WORK, BY TASK

Specification no.	Brief description	Frequency/ quantity	Unit	Hours estimated	Price quote (£)	Profit/ loss (£)
A123	Hedge cut	100	lin. m	16.00	300.00	
B456	Bowling-green cut	× 1	/green	1.40	33.33	
C678	Pavilion clean	× 1	/pav.	1.00	17.14	
		Totals				

Note: Figures are illustrative only.

ESTIMATING

Specification no.	Brief description	Frequency/ quantity	Unit	Hours estimated	Hourly rate (£)	+	Equipment/ materials (£)	Price/ quote (£)	Profit (£)
A123	Hedge cut	100	lin. m	16.00	17.00	+	1.75	300.00	
B456	Bowling-green cut	× 1	/green	1.40	18.00	+	2.00	33.33	
C678	Pavilion clean	× 1	/pav.	1.00	17.00	+	0.14	17.14	

ANALYSIS OF REGULAR/CYCLICAL WORK, BY TEAM

Week no. _____ Team no. _____ Date _____

Specification no.	Brief description	Location	Frequency/ quantity	Hours actually worked	Hours estimated	Price/ quote (£)	Cost Profit/loss (£)
A123	Hedge cut	KGV	500.00		80.00	1 500	
B456	Bowling-green cut	KGV	× 3		5.00	100	
C678	Pavilion clean	KGV	× 7		7.00	120	
		Totals		A	B	C	D

Team leader's signature _____ Date _____

Note:
B − A = the team's profit-and-loss situation, in workhours;
D − C = the team's profit-and-loss situation, in cash terms.
(Ensure that due allowance is made for absences, holidays, etc.)

Chapter Twelve

Conclusion

Amenity horticulture has traditionally operated within a very close master-servant relationship. In the landscaped and manicured gardens of a bygone era, the gardeners were not only directly employed by the family in the big house, they were in almost daily contact with them. They had to be. Amenity horticulture required daily supervision and direction.

CLOSE SUPERVISION

The public parks provided by the emerging municipalities of the Victorian era, proceeded in the same manner. Gardeners were directly employed and closely supervised. As greenkeeping was added to the list of tasks carried out under the Parks Department, direct contact continued.

It took many decades for the secrets of the potting-sheds to be revealed; for the fertilizer programme of a bowling-green to be standardized; and for the care of trees to be codified. But it has happened. Amenity horticulture in the 1990s is a far more standardized service than it was even 20 or 30 years ago.

UNIFORMITY

The final step is to codify the rest of amenity horticulture in all its many diverse aspects; this will be completed by the turn of the century. It will follow naturally from the introduction of competitive tendering. Whether that is desirable, is not now for debate: it will happen.

Clients will learn that contractors will carry out only that which is detailed in the specification or job instruction – and nothing more. That lesson will be learned the hard way. Hence clients will continually add more detail to their specifications and work instructions. Whole compendiums will be written. The transformation of amenity horticulture will be complete.

In addition, a close working relationship of a different nature will result. The regular contact will still be there; gardeners and groundsmen will still be paid; but all will have been formalized, written and codified. Payment will depend on satisfactory completion of the work.

The successful contractor who grapples with this new formality will be the real winner by the end of the decade. He will have seized and exploited the opportunities which the decade offers him.

SUCCESS VIA ADAPTABILITY

The many examples given throughout this book indicate that all companies start from small beginnings. Some stay small, some grow to become 'household names' within the horticultural industry. All have succeeded through attention to detail, and developing an intuitive knowledge of how to succeed in their own particular market niche.

This group of mainly private sector contractors will be increasingly joined by successful public sector contractor companies. They too will have adapted to, and grown with, the new environment. Some will have formed break-away contractor companies and will be competing right across the private sector of operation. Others will have become highly successful contractors still firmly attached to the parent public authority and, perhaps, winning contracts in neighbouring areas. There will be a natural ebb and flow in the life of contracts and contractors.

Maintenance by contract is, if nothing else, a very variable business. Many contracts will continue to their natural completion. Others will have difficulties and may be terminated before the end of the contract period.

It will be the same with contractors. Some will last the course, others will not. This will be equally true of public contractors as well as private contractors. The companies familiar to all at the beginning of the decade will not, perhaps, be the same at the end. Also in each locality contractors will have enjoyed, or otherwise, very different experiences.

As for the standard of service, that all depends on a number of factors. It will be immensely varied and variable in the first half of the decade of the 1990s. Thereafter, it should settle down; but given a willing contractor and client, there is no inherent reason why the standards could not be improved.

COSTS AND BENEFITS

Costs will be reduced – that is costs for the routine cyclical work, at least, will be reduced. This lends itself to an efficient contractor operation. Costs for the many one-off jobs will increase, as will the costs of supervision and office management procedures.

Provided that everyone benefits, client, contractor and most important of all, the customers (sports players or local residents), then the new order of maintenance should be welcomed. Improved service achieved at lower cost will be the real test of that new order.

The new order too will be fully operational by the start of the new century. Two thousand years and more of traditional methods will be gone. The craftsman will no longer pass on his trade and learning by hand. It will be all written down.

APPENDIX A: AN OUTLINE TENDER DOCUMENT

This appendix provides an outline of the main parts to be found in most tender documents. In addition to the outline, a few example clauses are given:

1. *Instructions for Tendering*
   A formal statement of how to go about submitting the tender.
2. *Form of Tender*
   Quite brief; this is the actual tender, the formal offer.
3. *Draft Form of Contract*
   Brief; this is the actual written contract, when signed.
4. *Conditions of Contract*
   The rules or conditions by which the contract will be operated.
5. *Form of Bond*
   A payment by the contractor, which then forms a financial bond between contractor and client.
6. *Form of Insurance*
   Covers the contractor for normal risks.
7. *Specification*
   Many pages of specific work instructions.
8. *Bill of Quantities*
   The actual quantity of work, which the contractor prices.
9. *Schedule of Rates*
   Works required, which are hard to quantify; also to be priced.
10. *Work Schedule or Programme*
    An example of work – how, when and where.
11. *Plans and Maps*
    Plans of all sites to be maintained.
12. *Parent Company Indemnity*
    Where a small subsidiary company wins a contract this form will ensure that the parent company is responsible for any costs arising through the failure of that smaller company.

APPENDIX A1: INSTRUCTIONS FOR TENDERING

These instructions will give a formal guide to the completion of the tender document. Instructions will vary from one tender to the next.

1. Invitation to the contractor.
2. Preparations by the contractor.
2.1. The contractor will be made responsible, entirely at his own expense, for obtaining all the information required to complete the tender.
2.2. When completed, the tender document will returned in its entirety to the client. Hence two copies of the tender document are normally supplied to the contractor, so that he may retain one.
2.3. The contractor will be required to meet the client and discuss details.
2.4. Pricing will be in pounds sterling, and two decimal places.
2.5. Any inquiries relating to any part of the tender document should be made in writing to the client. At his absolute discretion, the client may amend or alter the tender document, by giving written notification to all the contractors invited to tender.
3. Additional information to be provided.
3.1. The contractor will enclose a copy of his current Health and Safety policy with the tender.
3.2. The contractor is also to supply an outline of the contractor's working methods that is:

  - itemized list of vehicles, plant, equipment;
  - type, quantity and abilities of manpower;
  - a general description of working methods.

4. Submission of the tender by the contractor. The completed tender must be submitted by 12 noon on the stated date. *Note*: A tender submitted even one minute late will be declared null and void.
5. Acceptance and publication.
5.1. The authority does not bind itself to accept the lowest – or indeed any – tender.
5.2. The authority will publish the value of all tenders, and the names of all tenderers.

APPENDIX A2: FORM OF TENDER

The following example is the actual formal offer (or tender) from the contractor to the client.

PUBLIC AUTHORITY XYZ

GROUNDS MAINTENANCE TENDER

To the members of Public Authority XYZ
Address:

Ladies and Gentlemen

Having examined all the tender documents contained herein, we offer to undertake all the works at the price stated, for a period of four years.

We agree that within one calendar month of the acceptance of this tender, we will:
— enter into a formal Agreement which will bind us contractually to undertake the priced works for four years;
— enter into a formal performance bond;
— provide all financial information requested about our company.

We accept that you are not bound to accept the lowest or any tender.

We are, Ladies and Gentlemen

Name of Company: _____

Authorized signatures: _____

_____

(authorized by the Company to sign
on behalf of the Company)

PRINT NAMES IN FULL _____

_____

Address:

Date:

Your attention is particularly drawn to the 'Instructions for Tendering'. The tender is to be returned, sealed in the envelope provided, to the Authority's office, at the address stated above, before noon on _____. Tenders received after this time WILL NOT be considered.

APPENDIX A3: DRAFT FORM OF CONTRACT

The example given below provides a summary guideline to the type of contract which will be signed by both parties (client and contractor).

GROUNDS MAINTENANCE

This Agreement is made this day of _____
between Public Authority XYZ (referred to subsequently as 'the client') and Contractor ABC (referred to subsequently as 'the contractor').

The client has accepted the tender submitted by the contractor, for the grounds maintenance works within the Authority's area for a period of 4 years from _____ (date).

All the documents contained within the tender numbered 1 to 12, together with any other documents/letters stated, will now form part of this Agreement.

The contractor hereby undertakes to carry out all the works as stated in all these combined documents to the satisfaction of the client.

The client hereby undertakes to pay the contractor the agreed payments, at the frequency, and in the manner, stated in the conditions.

Signed:
(for the client)
Mayor: _____
Witness: _____

(for the contractor)
Director: _____
Witness: _____

APPENDIX A4: CONDITIONS OF CONTRACT

The conditions stated here only cover, in brief outline, some of the more important conditions of contract, which will frequently occur.

1. Definitions
   (a) Client: the Public Authority XYZ.
   (b) Contractor: the company or individual who submitted the tender which has been accepted.
   (c) Clerk of Works: the officer of the client who has been duly introduced to the contractor as Clerk of Works.
   (d) (All other important, frequently occurring terms will be defined.)
2. Contract period
Four years, with an option for an extra two years.
3. Sites
The sites will be as stated in the plans and maps, included in the tender document, as varied only by written notification from the client.
4. Measurements
The measurements of all the sites will be as specified in the Bill of Quantities. In the event of a dispute of any specific site, an exact measurement of the site will be made, with representatives of both parties present. If the site measurement reveals an error of more than 5%, the measurement within the Bill of Quantities will be changed accordingly.
5. Quality of service
The quality of service will be entirely in accordance with the specification, and to the satisfaction of the client and his Clerk of Works.
6. Payments
The contractor will submit to the client, at the end of each month, a detailed invoice, stating the sums to which the contractor considers himself entitled (including any variation agreed in writing by the client). The client will pay all agreed invoices within one calendar month thereafter.
7. Staff
   (a) Only able and competent staff will be employed by the contractor.
   (b) ...race relations.
   (c) ...health and safety at work.
   (d) ...identification of staff.
   (e) ...etc.
8. Supervision
9. British Standards
10. Hours of working allowed
11. Indemnity and insurance
12. Annual price increase allowed for inflation
13. Assignment
Assignment of this contract, in part or in full, will not be allowed unless specific prior written permission has been given by the client to another named contractor.
14. Termination
The client will be allowed to terminate the contract if:
   (a) the contractor has offered or accepted any inducement in attempting to secure the contract.
   (b) the contractor commits any breach of obligation as stated in this contract.
   (c) the contractor becomes bankrupt, or insolvent, or goes into receivership
And if the contract is terminated, then:

(d) the client is permitted to employ other contractors to undertake the works, entirely at the expense of the original contractor; this expense will form a debt on that contractor.

15. Arbitration

Where a dispute exists between the client and contractor, and it cannot be satisfactorily settled by negotiation between the two parties, the matter will be referred to an independent Arbitrator to obtain a decision.

APPENDIX A5: FORM OF BOND

The bond will literally bond a third party to cover any costs resulting from poor performance by the contractor, where the contractor is unable to meet these costs himself. Again, only an outline bond is given here.

By this bond, we the contractor whose registered office is at _____ and the financial company/bank/insurance company, whose registered office is at _____ are bound to the Public Authority XYZ to the value of £

It be hereby understood by both parties that the Contractor has entered into a contract with Public Authority XYZ for the provision of grounds maintenance services totally in accordance with the contract documents.

The Conditions of the Bond are that if the Contractor does not satisfy all or part of the contract, then the financial company/bank/insurance company will meet the costs incurred by Public Authority XYZ to the full amount of this Bond.

Signed:
(for the financial company)
Director: _____
Witness: _____

Signed:
(for the contractor)
Director: _____
Witness: _____

APPENDIX A6: FORM OF INSURANCE

This form, when duly completed, provides evidence to the client as to the exact insurance cover being provided to the contractor. In the event of any claim resulting during the operation of the contract, the contractor's costs are to be fully covered. The indemnity ensures that the responsibility rests entirely with the contractor, and not the client.

To the Members of Public Authority XYZ
Address:

This is to certify that
Contractor: _____
who is to undertake the grounds maintenance contract for Public Authority XYZ is covered in respect of all risks referred to within the Conditions of Contract.

The Policy number is: _____
and expiry date is: _____

The limit of liability for any one accident is at least £5 000 000.

Insurers: _____
Address: _____

Authorized signature: _____

(authorized by the Insurance
Company to sign on behalf
of the Company)

PRINT NAME IN FULL _____
Witness: _____
Date: _____

APPENDIX A7: SPECIFICATION

There will be many pages of detailed instructions specifying exactly how to carry out all the works. The example given in this appendix is reproduced from 'ILAM Competitive Tendering: Maintenance of Grounds and Open Spaces' (published by Longman).

II C-14 Grass cutting

14.1 *General*

(i) All grass will be cut cleanly and evenly, to the same height on each site and without damaging the existing surface.

(ii) The Contractor will notify the Supervising Officer of the machines he proposes to use on each site by completing the appropriate list and submitting it as part of his tender.

(iii) The Contractor will follow and keep to an approved system of cut to ensure that all areas are cut on a rota basis where applicable (e.g. housing estates). Any rota must be approved, before work commences, by the Supervising Officer.

(iv) The Contractor will complete one area of grasscutting before moving onto the next.

(v) Soft vegetative growth, such as clover, will be deemed to be part of the Contract where it falls within larger areas of grass.

(vi) The Contractor may be required to treat molehills and will ensure that he can provide the necessary staff, labour and materials for so doing.

(vii) Since it is not possible to predict accurately the precise number of mowings which may be required on any site in any one year, the Bill of Quantities includes a given number of mowings, but the Contractor will be paid on a pro-rata basis for more or less than this number, dependent upon the prevailing weather conditions throughout the growing season.

(viii) Mowing will take place on the full area of grass at the site, up to the paving, fencing and any other boundaries.

(ix) The Contractor will be required to recut any area, deemed to be unsatisfactorily mown, at his own expense.

(x) If inclement weather prevents the Contractor from mowing he will quickly resume grasscutting once the conditions become suitable again. The Contractor will be expected to provide sufficient manpower and machinery to catch up if there is a substantial amount of mowing time lost through bad weather.

(xi) Prior to cutting any area, the Contractor will remove all significantly large stones, as well as any paper, tins, bottles and other debris. All such material will be removed to a suitable, previously agreed tip. If the amount to be removed is considered excessive by the Contractor, he will inform immediately the Supervising Officer, who will consider each site on its individual merit and may agree to extra payments in exceptional circumstances.

(xii) The Contractor may be required to cut grass on new housing estates and other areas yet to be developed. He must ensure that he has sufficient resources to take on this extra cutting if required.

(xiii) In conditions of drought, the Contractor will ask the Supervising Officer to stipulate the height he wishes the height of cut to be raised to on each site.

(xiv) In very wet conditions, all operations involving grass cutting shall cease, until conditions allow operations to continue without:

– damaging the surface, levels and contours of the ground;

– creating grass cutting 'divots' from the rollers or cutters.

If the very wet conditions persist and additional operations are required to cut grass and remove arisings, then the Contractor will agree with the Supervising Officer a fair and reasonable rate for dealing with the excess growth.

(xv) In areas that contain bulbs or corms, the Contractor will arrange for grasscutting to be undertaken just prior to the emergence of the leaves in Spring. These areas will not be cut again until an instruction is received from the Supervising Officer. The cuttings arising will all be collected and disposed of at a suitable, previously agreed tip.

(xvi) The Contractor will remove all grass clippings arising from mowing from paved areas, mowing margins, channels, etc., by a method approved by the Supervising Officer. Generally this will be by sweeping or by the use of a 'blower'.

(xvii) All persons operating grasscutting machinery must be satisfactorily trained, and the Supervising Officer reserves the right to ask the Contractor to provide adequate proof that his operators are well trained, conversant with Health and Safety legislation and competent in their operating methods.

14.2 *Strimming*

(i) It will be necessary to cut grass around obstacles to the same height, frequency and standard as the surrounding grass areas. The Contractor will, therefore, provide within his grasscutting rate for strimming (or shearing) around such obstacles.

(ii) All arisings will be removed to a suitable, previously agreed tip.

14.3 *Other Associated Works*

(i) At each mowing visit, the Contractor will ensure that tree bases and other obstacles are clean, tidy and weedfree. His rate for grasscutting will, therefore, include for this associated work.

14.4 *Hooking*

The Contractor will be required to hook areas that are too steep or too thickly vegetated to be cut by mower or strimmer.

(i) The operator will wear appropriate protective clothing and will not endager himself or the public. He will be suitably roped or harnessed if the bank is steeper than 30° to the vertical. On such banks, two operators must always work together in case of injury.

(ii) All arisings will be removed to a suitable, previously agreed tip.

(iii) The finished site must look tidy and evenly cut to a maximum height of ......mm.

14.5 *List of machines to be used*

Site	Grass collected	Machine	Cutting Height	Maximum growth height
Bowling-greens	Yes			
Hockey fields	No			
Tennis courts	Yes			
Rough cut areas	No			
etc.	Etc.			

Client note: The Client is advised to complete the list of sites above (appropriate to his/her appropriate situation) together with the required heights. Be careful to be specific, e.g. cricket square, cricket wicket and cricket outfield, will all require different machines and cutting heights.

The Contractor will complete the above list by inserting the machines he proposes to use on each of the sites. This completed form will be deemed to form part of the Tender and must be wholly completed and submitted along with the priced Tender Documents.

The Contractor will list below all the grasscutting machinery available to him and the facilities he has available for maintaining the machinery in good, clean, working order.

An example table is provided at 14.6

14.6 *Example of completed table*

Area	Height of cut min.–max.		Machine	Frequency and directions for cutting
	mm	mm		
Bowls	4	8	10/12 bladed cylinder (variable speed)	Every Mon.–Wed.–Fri. in two directions at 90° to each other. Diagonally only during the playing season
Hockey, cricket outfield, croquet, golf fairway, lawn tennis. }	12	25	6 bladed cylinder (gang mowers)	Once per week. Each week at 90° to the previous week.
Football	15	30	6 bladed cylinder (gang mowers)	Once per week. Each week at 90° to the previous week.
Rugby	20	40	6 bladed cylinder (gang mowers)	Once per week. Each week at 90° to the previous week.
Golf: green	3	6	10/12 bladed cylinder	Every Mon.–Wed.–Fri. in two directions at 90° to each other
semi-rough	40	80	Rotary	
rough		80+	Rotary/flail	Once every month
Cricket: square	8	12	10/12 bladed cylinder (variable speed)	Every Mon.–Wed.–Fri. in two directions at 90°. As required for matches
wicket }	2	4		
Housing estates, highway verges	20	40	Cylinder or rotary	Once per week.
Rough-cut areas	100+		Pedestrian or tractor flail	Three times per year.

Client note: The height of cut is a suggest figure, but it will require altering in accordance with any changes in the proposed frequency for cutting.

Figures given are for the height of the growing season.
Figures may therefore be reduced as growth slows down on housing estates, verges, football pitches, etc.

Cuts per linear meter may also be stated in the 'Machine' column to further define the quality of cut desired.

APPENDIX A8: BILL OF QUANTITIES

The Bill of Quantities quantifies the workload. Furthermore, it is this section which is priced by the contractor. When all the prices have been added together, the largest proportion of the value of the tender will have been calculated. There are additional items, such as the Schedule of Rates, which appears in Appendix A9.

Item no.	Description	Total quantity	Unit	Rate (£)	Annual frequency	Annual price
A123	Hedge cut	10 500	lin. m		× 2	
B456	Bowling-green cut	10	/green		× 78	
C678	Pavilion clean	20	/pav.		× 156	
D987	Litter	all. . .	sites		× 52	
E654	Triple mow	100	acre		× 26	
G234	Strim	all. . .	sites		× 26	
F321	Beds, cultivate	20 000	sq. m		× 2	
			Sub-total			£

Total – to be transferred to totals on final page

APPENDIX A9: SCHEDULE OF RATES

A schedule of the contractor's rates (or prices) will often be requested in addition to the Bill of Quantities. These tend to be for works which are not carried out very often. Thus they are therefore somewhat harder to quantify, and consequently price. Sometimes the total tender is based on a Schedule of Rates.

Item no.	Brief description	Unit of measurement	Rate (£.p)
R.1	Provision of the manager	per hour	
R.2	Provision of a supervisor	per hour	
R.3	Provision of a gardener or groundsman	per hour	
R.4	Provision of a tractor, 5-gang mower and driver	per hour	
R.5	Provision of a triple mower and driver	per hour	
R.6	Repair of fence (chain link) with 10% defects	per 100 m^2	
R.7	Hand weed between cobbles	100 m^2	
R.8	Hand brush a paved area	100 m^2	
R.9	Clear a clothes drying area of all weeds, moss and debris. Treat with approved chemical weedkiller. Leave clean and tidy	100 m^2	
R.10	Provide supervisors and 10 men on a Sunday, to work as directed (e.g. at a special show or event) NB: This rate may be used pro rata, for more or less than 10 men, and for more or less than 10 hours	Per 10 hour	

APPENDIX A10: WORK SCHEDULE

The key to continuing success is an efficiently organized work schedule or programme, which will expeditiously undertake all the routine regular work. This may be provided by the client. Alternatively, this information may need to be submitted by the contractor. The best work programmes are jointly agreed between contractor and client.

The Contractor is to provide here, a clear indication of his methods of working. Taking one team or one area of work, detail the methods of working to be undertaken on a stated regular workload, as detailed in the tender documents.

Area of work: _____
Manpower to be employed: _____
_____

Machinery to be used: _____
_____
_____

Commencing work at: _____
Finishing work at: _____
Estimated time taken (in days): _____
Any other details: _____
_____
_____

This work programme is to provide an indication of the manner in which the contractor will carry out the work, if offered a contract. This programme will also form the basis of discussions with the client during the tender period.

APPENDIX A11: MAPS AND PLANS

A variety of maps and plans will be provided with most tender documents. Location plans will indicate the principal parks, open spaces and playing-fields; and any natural divisions within the town (e.g. East and West) which the client wishes to emphasize.

The example given below of a town plan, is reproduced from the Audit Commission publication. Competitive Management of Parks and Green Spaces 1990.

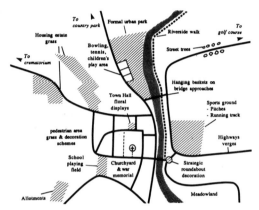

In addition, example plans will be provided, indicating the exact location of the actual work areas – e.g. hedges, flower beds and grass areas. To ensure that no small sites are missed, the plans will be very detailed in some places.

The example plan below is provided by permission of System Design for Micros Ltd/Treekno.

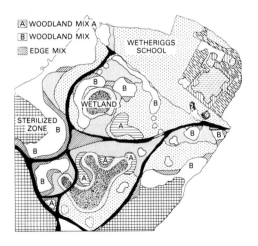

APPENDIX A12: PARENT COMPANY INDEMNITY

Where a subsidiary company is to undertake a contract, the client will wish to ensure that it has sufficient capability and financial resources to fulfil its obligations. There is no better method open to the client than to require a formal and binding statement from the parent company.

This Agreement is made this day of _____
between Public Authority XYZ (referred to subsequently as 'the client') and Company ABC (referred to subsequently as 'the parent company').

Whereas the client has entered into a contract with contractor A, the parent company has now agreed to indemnify the client in the event of any failure of due performance by contractor A, howsoever caused.

The indemnity is to cover any and all losses, claims, costs, expenses or damages, howsoever arising – being due to the breach of any part of the contract between the client and contractor, and entirely in accordance with the contract between the client and contractor A.

Should this indemnity come into operation, the parent company will be bound entirely by the totality of the contract, without variation, between the client and contractor A.

Signed:
(for the client)
Mayor: _____
Witness: _____
Date: _____
(for the parent company)
Director: _____
Witness: _____
Date: _____

APPENDIX B: SOME USEFUL BRITISH STANDARDS

The importance of British Standards will increase as maintenance by contract becomes more routine.

The use of appropriate British Standards will also indicate the hallmark of the professional landscape contractor.

BS 1722: Part 1: 1986
Specification for chain link fences.
Requirements for chain link fences, and for gates and gateposts for use with chain link fences, up to 1.8 m high.

BS 1722: Part 2: 1973
Woven wire fences.
Construction, workmanship, erection of general pattern and high-tensile steel wire fences. Types, uses, construction details, sizes of components. Characteristics and permissible defects for softwoods and hardwoods. Preservative treatments.

BS 1722: Part 3: 1986
Specification for strained wire fences.
Fences of the general pattern and the dropper pattern.

BS 1722: Part 4: 1986
Specification for cleft chestnut pale fences.
Fences constructed from cleft sweet chestnut supported by wires between sweet chestnut or concrete posts.

BS 1722: Part 5: 1986
Specification for close boarded fences.
Requirements for close boarded fences of oak and other timber from 1.05 to 1.8 m high.

BS 1722: Part 6: 1986
Specification for wooden palisade fences.
Fences with both rectangular and triangular palisades.

BS 1722: Part 7: 1986
Specification for wooden post and rail fences.
Fences of the morticed type and the nailed type.

BS 1722: Part 8: 1978
Mild steel (low-carbon) steel continuous bar fences.
Requirements for several types of fences, their construction and erection; details of materials and protective treatment.

BS 1722: Part 9: 1979
Mild steel (low-carbon steel) fences with round or square verticals and flat posts and horizontals.
Requirements for self-adjusting riveted and welded fences and for erection.

BS 1722: Part 10: 1972
Anti-intruder chain link fences.
Construction, dimensions, workmanship, erection for fences for individual security purposes such as factories, airfields, oilfields; includes PVC-covered wire, design of gates and posts; manufacture, maturing and testing of reinforced concrete posts and struts.

BS 1722: Part 11: 1986
Specification for woven wood and lap boarded panel fences.
Softwood panel fences with timber or concrete posts.

BS 1722: Part 12: 1979
Steel palisade fences.
Requirements for general purpose fences in corrugated and angled pales and for security fences in corrugated pales.

BS 1722: Part 13: 1978
Chain link fences for tennis court surrounds.
Minimum requirements for chain link fencing and posts.

BS 3882: 1965(1978)
Recommendations and classification for top soil.
Description of top soil, classification by texture, classification by soil reaction (pH); classification by stone content, size of stones; notes on method of test for top soil; designation of top soil.

BS 3936: Part 1: 1980
Specification for trees and shrubs.
Trees and shrubs, including conifers and woody climbing plants, suitable to be transplanted and grown for amenity; covers origin, root system, condition, dimensions, packaging and labelling and forms and sizes to be supplied for wide range of species.

BS 3936: Part 2: 1978
Roses.
Definitions and requirements for rootstocks, age, condition, trimming and dimensions of bush and shrub, climbing, rambling and pillar, standards, half-standards and weeping standards, dwarf and miniature roses, packaging and labelling.

BS 3936: Part 3: 1978
Fruit.
Origin, root system and rootstock, form of trees (illustrated), condition, packaging, certification and plant health; labelling requirements for apples, pears, cherries, plums, peaches, nectarines and apricots, blackcurrants, red currants and whitecurrants, gooseberries, raspberries, blackberries and loganberries and strawberries.

BS 3936: Part 4: 1984
Specification for forest trees.
Requirements for origin, dimensions, root and shoot, description, condition and packaging of forest trees for timber production.

BS 3936: Part 5: 1985
Specification for poplars and willows.
Specifies requirements for dimensions, shoot condition and marking for plants to be grown for timber production, shelter belts or for amenity.

BS 3936: Part 7: 1989
Specification for bedding plants.
Origin, growing medium, number of plants in a box, gaps, condition, planting dates, labelling; applies to the most common ranges of ornamental plants and vegetables grown and sold for planting out directly into open ground.

BS 3936: Part 9: 1987
Specification for bulbs, corms and tubers.
Dimensions, condition, time of flowering and labelling of the more commonly grown plants.

BS 3936: Part 10: 1981
Specification for ground cover plants.
Definitions and requirements for origin, root system, condition, dimensions, packaging, designation and labelling; appendix gives information about minimum spread of 101 types of plant and indication of whether they are deciduous, evergreen or herbaceous.

BS 3936: Part 11: 1984
Specification for container-grown culinary herbs.
Definition, requirements for root-system, dimensions, designation and labelling; appendix gives common and botanical names of 30 plants and indicates whether they are annual, biennial or perennial and hardy or half-hardy.

BS 3969: 1965 (1978)
Recommendations for turf for general landscape purposes.
Common and botanical names of grasses and perennial weeds;

constituent desirable grasses, undesirable grasses and weeds, soil, condition, dimensions of turves, delivery.

BS 3998: 1966
Recommendations for tree work.
Safety, season and equipment, workmanship, inspection; individual operations, cuts, pruning, lifting of crown, cleaning out, crown thinning, reducing and reshaping, restoration, repair work, bracing, feeding, tree removal; appendices cover safety precautions, season, method for protecting a large tree to be used as an anchor, three methods for feeding trees after tree work, examples of methods for treatment of roots with ammonium sulphamate or sodium chlorate.

BS 4043: 1966 (1978)
Recommendations for transplanting semi-mature trees.
Selection of trees for transplanting, season for transplanting, preparation by root pruning; tree pits, drainage, tree lifting operations; lifting, loading and transporting, planting, backfilling and mulching, operational damage; guying and securing the tree, wrapping, watering and spraying; appendices classifying trees suitable for transplanting, giving guidance as to the size of prepared root systems, and with examples of guying and securing techniques.

BS 4156: 1967
Specification for peat.
Peat produced for general horticulture and landscape purposes; requirements as to pH, moisture content, ash, particle size, yield (volume out) and marking.

BS 4428: 1969
Recommendations for general landscape operations (excluding hard surfaces).
Deals with the following general landscape operations: preparatory operations, including earthwork, land shaping and drainage; seeding of grass areas; turfing; planting of shrubs, hedges, climbers, herbaceous plants and bulbs; individual tree planting; forestry planting for amenity purposes.

BS 4746: 1971
Recommendations for the location and direction of movement of controls of pedestrian-operated tractors, agricultural and horticultural machines.
Details recommendations for the location and direction of motion of the principal controls for pedestrian-operated tractors, rotary cultivators, motor-hoes, motor-scythes, and similar small pedestrian-operated powered agricultural and horticultural machines; includes recommendations regarding the marking of specified controls.

BS 5236: 1975
Recommendations for the cultivation and planting of trees in the advanced nursery stock category.
Recommendations for description, production, preparation for sale, packaging, labelling, planting, mulching and staking; recommendations on the dimensions for trees sold in the form of standards.

BS 5696: Part 3: 1979
Code of practice for installation and maintenance.
Gives recommendations for the installation and maintenance of outdoor play equipment intended for public use; includes guidance on siting and layout. (This standard is being considered for approval under the Approval of Safety Standards Regulations 1987.)

BS 5701: 1980
Guide to number-defective charts for quality control.
Describes the simplest method of statistical quality control by examination for the number of defectives in samples taken from a process that produces individual units of product rather than a continuous product; accepted methods of charting which are easy to use and may safely and profitably replace 100% routine examinations. Replaces BS 1313: 1974.

BS 5750: Part 0:
Principal concepts and applications.

BS 5750: Part 0: Section 0.1: 1987
Guide to selection and use.
Clarifies the principal quality concepts and provides guidance on the selection and use of the BS 5750 series of standards on quality systems that can be used for internal quality management purposes and for external quality assurance purposes.

BS 5750: Part 0: Section 0.2: 1987
Guide to quality management and quality system elements.
Describes a basic set of elements by which quality systems can be developed and implemented, for internal quality management purposes; the selection of appropriate elements and the extent to which these elements are adopted and applied by a company will depend upon factors such as market being served, nature of product, production process and consumer needs.

BS 5750: Part 1: 1987
Specification for design/development, production, installation and servicing.
Quality system requirements for use where a contract between two

parties requires the demonstration of a supplier's capability to design and supply a product or service.

BS 5750: Part 2: 1987
Specification for production and installation.
Quality system requirements for use where a contract between two parties requires demonstration of a supplier's capability to control the processes that determine the acceptability of the product or service supplied.

BS 5750: Part 3: 1987
Specification for final inspection and test.
Quality system requirements for use where a contract between two parties requires demonstration of a supplier's capability to detect and control the disposition of any product non-conformity during final inspection and test.

BS 5750: Part 4: 1981
Guide to the use of BS 5750: Part 1, 'Specification for design, manufacture and installation'.
Provides guidance on the implementation of Part 1 of the Standard, aimed at affording a better understanding of the specification itself, as well as assistance in its use, either in implementing or in evaluating such assistance.

BS 5750: Part 5: 1981
Guide to the use of BS 5750: Part 2, 'Specification for manufacture and installation'.
Provides guidance on the implementation of Part 2 of the Standard, aimed at affording a better understanding of the specification itself, as well as assistance in its use, either in implementing or in evaluating such assistance.

BS 5750: Part 6: 1981
Guide to the use of BS 5750: Part 3, 'Specification for final inspection and test'.
Provides guidance on the implementation of Part 3 of the Standard, aimed at affording a better understanding of the specification itself, as well as assistance in its use, either in implementing or in evaluating such assistance.

BS 5837: 1980
Code of practice for trees in relation to construction.
Principles to follow to achieve satisfactory juxtaposition of trees and construction; recommends types of trees for planting near buildings,

structures, plant and services; advice on planting and maintenance of trees in urban locations and paved areas.

The British Standards Institute is currently considering a standard for grounds maintenance. Part I is expected to cover: principles, organization and management, planning factors.

British Standards are updated from time to time, and some stated in the above list are currently being revised.

Inquiries in relation to British Standards should be addressed to:

BSI Enquiry Section,
Linford Wood,
Milton Keynes,
MK14 6LE
Tel. 0908 221166
(call queueing system
in operation)

For sales, use the same address, but orders to the Sales Department.

APPENDIX C: ACKNOWLEDGEMENTS AND REFERENCES

This appendix provides a comprehensive list of the various sources of information used in the book. My gratitude is expressed to all who helped in the compilation of this book.

Aramis Computing Services Ltd
Salford House,
2 Evesham Street,
Alcester,
Warwickshire, B49 5DN

A computer systems supplier with specific reference to grounds maintenance by competitive tendering. The systems have been developed in conjunction with The Groundswork Trust. Acknowledgement is given for the illustrative extracts provided within this book.

The Audit Commission for Local Authorities
in England and Wales
1 Vincent Square,
London SW1P 2PN

Grateful acknowledgement is given to The Audit Commission, and to the Controller of Her Majesty's Stationery Office, for various illustrations and extracts throughout this book, and especially from the publications entitled, *Competitive Management of Parks and Green Spaces* 1988, and *Preparing for Compulsory Competition* 1989. These publications may be purchased from Her Majesty's Stationery Office, at the address given below.

British Association of Landscape Industries
Landscape House,
9 Henry Street,
Keighley,
West Yorkshire BD21 3DR

Acknowledgement is given for the help and advice of the British Association of Landscape Industries, in particular their publication; *BALI; Who's Who 1989.*

British Standards Institute
Linford Wood,
Milton Keynes MK14 6LE

Acknowledgement is given to the British Standards Institute for the list of appropriate Standards detailed in Appendix B.

Contractor Services Group (Bath) Ltd
Newton Road,
Twerton,
Bath BA2 9JQ

Acknowledgement is given for the informative help of the Contractor Services Group (Bath) Ltd in relation to their background, current and future prospects and their general business philosophy.

Her Majesty's Stationery Office
(Publications Division – Copyright)

Material from the Audit Commission (listed above), the Local Government Act 1988, Department of Environment Circulars 8/88 and 19/88, reproduced by permission of the Controller of Her Majesty's Stationery Office. Publications are available by post or telephone from:

HMSO Publications Centre
PO Box 276,
London SW8 5DT
Tel. 071-873 9090
General inquiries: 071-873 0011
or through HMSO Bookshop or accredited agents (see Yellow Pages) and other good bookshops.

Horticultural Trades Association
19 High Street,
Theale,
Reading,
Berkshire RG7 5AH

Acknowledgement is given for the use of their standard form of tender for 'The Supply and Delivery of Plants'.

The Institute of Leisure and Amenity Management
Lower Basildon,
Reading,
Berkshire RG8 9NE

Grateful acknowledgement is given to ILAM and their authors for the extracts from *ILAM Competitive Tendering: Maintenance of Grounds and Open Spaces* 1988.

The Institute of Quality Assurance
10 Grosvenor Gardens,
London SW1 0DQ

Grateful acknowledgement is given to The Institute of Quality Assurance, for their document 'Quality Assurance, Cleansing Services, Grounds Maintenance and Leisure Facilities'.

The Joint Council for Landscape Industries
15 Carlton House Terrace,
London SW1Y 5AH

Acknowledgement for the use of the JCL1 Standard Form of Contract, which the JCLI wishes to be used as widely as possible.

The Longman (Publishing) Group (UK) Ltd
6th Floor,
Westgate House,
The High,
Harlow,
Essex CM20 1YR

Acknowledgement is due for the extracts from *ILAM Competitive Tendering: Maintenance of Grounds and Open Spaces* 1988.

Parkfield Landscapes
Broad Lane,
Engine Common,
Yate,
Bristol BS17 5PN

Acknowledgement is due for freely given information about the experiences of Parkfield Landscapes in the new environment.

Public Sector Services
72 West Parade,
Lincoln LN1 1JY

Kind acknowledgement is given for the extracts used in relation to time and cost management, and for their consultancy advice, given at seminars and workshop sessions.

Systems Design for Micros Ltd/Treekno
3a Newton Court,
Wavertree Technology Park,
Liverpool L13 1EJ

Acknowledgement is given to Systems Design for Micros Ltd/ Treekno, for permission to reproduce the plan in Appendix A11.

Tyler Environmental Services Ltd
Nuthampstead,
Barkway,
Royston,
Hertfordshire SG8 8LZ

Acknowledgement is given for the details provided about their origins, development and growth over almost 30 years.

T.P. Ulyett Landscapes
Main Street,
Bidworth,
Mansfield,
Nottinghamshire NG21 OPX

Grateful acknowledgement is given for the insight into his experiences with a number of nearby local authorities.

I should like to record my gratitude to everyone who has helped in the production of this book, whether listed above or not. The book was only made possible through the widespread and generous support freely given by so many.

Index